Speaking
Is An Audience-Centered Sport

Books by Marjorie Brody, CSP

Power Presentations:
How To Connect With Your Audience
& Sell Your Ideas

•

Complete Business Etiquette Handbook

•

Business Etiquette

•

Climbing The Corporate Ladder

•

Minding Your Business Manners

•

Speaking Is An Audience-Centered Sport

•

Speaking Your Way To The Top:
Making Powerful Business Presentations

•

21 Ways To Springboard Your Speaking,
Training & Consulting Career

Speaking
Is An Audience-Centered Sport

Marjorie Brody, CSP
(Certified Speaking Professional)

Career Skills Press

Speaking Is An Audience-Centered Sport

Marjorie Brody, CSP

Copy Editors: Aren Alfaro, Miryam S. Roddy
Cover Design & Layout: Foster & Foster, Inc.
and Christos Christou

Copyright © 1998 Career Skills Press
Printed in the United States of America

Published by
Career Skills Press
P.O. Box 8868
Elkins Park, PA 19027
1-800-726-7936
Tel.: 215-886-1688
Fax: 215-886-1699
E-mail: brodycomm@brodycomm.com
http://www.brodycomm.com

Library of Congress Cataloging-in-Publication
Data in Process

ISBN: 0-9654827-2-3

I want to thank Aren Alfaro for her words; Miryam S. Roddy for her editing; and Dr. Alan Frieman, Julie Muchnick, Amy Brody, and Bill Steele for their photographic participation.

I'd also like to acknowledge the pros who contributed to this book, Brody Communications Ltd. staff, and all the clients that I have trained and coached for more than 20 years.

For more information on Marjorie Brody's keynotes
and Brody Communications Ltd. programs and
learning tools, write to:
P.O. Box 8868, Elkins Park, PA 19027
Visit our home page on the World Wide Web at:
http://www.brodycomm.com
Call us toll-free: 1-800-726-7936,
or 215-886-1688,
or fax us:215-886-1699
You can also e-mail us at:
brodycomm@brodycomm.com

Table of Contents

WHAT OTHER SUCCESSFUL AUTHORS, SPEAKERS, TRAINERS & CONSULTANTS ARE SAYING ABOUT THIS BOOK

"If you want your stand-up presentations to stand out, Marjorie Brody's book is a must read."

— **Jim Meisenheimer, CSP,** author of *50 More Ways to Sell Smarter*

"You are right on! Speaking and presentation skills are vital. Too many smart people work with one hand tied behind their backs because they do not make outstanding presentations. Thank you for making this vital subject the focus of a practical, easy to use book."

— **Dr. Revenue, John S. Haskell,** professional speaker/marketing and sales consultant, Los Angeles

"Your career or marketplace advantage comes from your ability to sell yourself and your ideas. Marjorie Brody has put it together for you in a practical way and from a street-smart perspective. Whether you're communicating with one person or a group, you'll stand out from the crowd after reading her collection of concepts, strategies and ideas."

— **Mark LeBlanc,** Resource, Small Business Success

"Marjorie Brody is a master presenter who will teach even the most timid amateur into a polished platform professional."

— **Jeffrey W. Hayzlett,** professional speaker and author

"I recently read in the Wall Street Journal *that good presentation skills were the #1 requirement for an organizational leader in today's business world. Marjorie has given you all the tools to give an excellent presentation. Now you must give your presentation the passion and spirit of conviction that will score the winning touchdown. You are learning from the best in the communication business — a cheerleader, coach, and quarterback extraordinaire."*

— **Barbara Glanz,** author of *Care Packages for the Workplace*

"Outside the privacy of your own home, all speaking is 'public speaking.' There is no skill that will help you leapfrog ahead in your career more than learning to speak eloquently. Marjorie Brody's book Speaking Is An Audience-Centered Sport *is a great way to get started on your journey to competence."*

Patricia Fripp, CSP, CPAE, Past President, National Speakers Association

"Powerful, practical, positive. A MUST READ. I can't tell you how many times this information could have benefited me as a corporate officer in a $600 million company. I plan to make Speaking Is An Audience-Centered Sport *mandatory reading for each member of my firm. It will be a powerful resource for corporate executives and salespeople for many years to come."*

— **Bill Lee, CSP,** President of Lee Resources Inc.

Part One

Why You Need This Book

"Each day you get to make a choice whether you are going to take a step forward, remain the same, or take a step back."
— Kirk McCaskill, Chicago White Sox

During the many years I spent teaching speech and rhetoric at a college, and in the years since as president of Brody Communications Ltd., I developed my philosophy that "life is a presentation."

Whether you have chosen a career in business, public service, sales, teaching, medicine, computer technology, or whatever the direction or goals you have, you will be presenting yourself, and your ideas, to others. From going on job interviews to making sales calls, from attending staff meetings to giving full-scale multimedia presentations, your ability to present with confidence and competence will have great impact on your career.

In today's fast-changing business environment, you may find yourself face-to-face with clients or customers thousands of miles from your office doing business through video conferences. Or, you might find yourself

1

working from home delivering your presentations on the telephone or through the computer. Expectations run high in a climate where technology changes as quickly as the seasons of the year.

Business presentations fall into several categories. Speeches are what most people think of when they hear the word presentation. But presentations are much more. They encompass all types of meetings, sales calls, customer service calls, sales pitches to acquire additional business or new clients, and even job interviews. In a large company, there may be hundreds of presentations in its various departments and sites. In even the smallest business, there may be two or three: the boss giving a status report before the office opens, a report on a client meeting or results of research. All are presentations.

In today's ever-changing business world, the best communicator may be the one who keeps his or her job during a downsizing. The knockout speaker will impress clients and customers far more often than even the best-written report. You need the edge that becoming a polished presenter offers. Whether you will use that edge to become more visible in your company, your community or your industry, is up to you. I offer you the tools to help you achieve your own success.

From the initial steps you must take to organize your presentation through the collection of data, models of organization, writing your presentation, practicing properly, developing good platform skills, and conquering your stage fright, right up to the final question-and-answer period, everything you need to know to develop your own audience-centered presentations is here for you. Most people (and books) focus on the speaker, when, in fact, the whole event should be centered on the audience. The speaker could be terrific, but if the particular audience, be it an audience of one or of one thousand, doesn't connect with or get involved with the speaker, the presentation won't work. There is no one style that will work all the time, because there is no one type of audience. There is no right way to speak. Speaking is an art, not a science.

As in professional sports, speakers, like athletes, must be mentally and physically ready to meet their challenges (the audience), they must know their material, and they must know the rules. As you develop your presentations, remember that speaking is an audience-centered sport. Refer to the chapters you need most. And, above all, don't be discouraged if your first presentations are not exactly what you wanted them to be. Even professional speakers have less than perfect performances – but like them, you may be the only one in the room who doesn't think your performance was all it could have been. Keep practicing, and keep presenting so that you will win your game. Good luck.

Part Two

The Preparation Process

"A pitcher should never 'throw' the ball; he should make a pitch. A pitch has a purpose and a target."
– **Bert Blyleven,** professional baseball player

Getting to know your PAL™

Before beginning to prepare for any presentation, it is crucial that you take your PAL™ into consideration. This PAL™ will be your best friend as you begin the process of learning to become a successful, audience-centered speaker. Your PAL™ stands for the three primary presentation considerations: **Purpose, Audience, Logistics.** Without a thorough analysis of all three, your chances for success will be considerably reduced. You may already know some general information about who your audience is even before you know the topic, but for the preparation process, your first concern will be to establish the purpose of your presentation.

Purpose

Your presentation will usually fall into one of three types of purposes: to inform, to persuade or to entertain. Before beginning the preparation of your presentation, you must find out or decide which type it will be.

The Informative Speech is given to share information with others. Your material must be interesting enough to capture the audience's attention, and presented in an interesting way to enable listeners to retain as much of it as possible. The amount of information that is retained will decrease as your presentation continues, so that by the end a great deal of it will not be remembered. However, by reinforcing your key ideas throughout the presentation, by incorporating visual aids, by involving the audience, by using stories and examples, by summarizing your key points at the end, and by the use of well-prepared handouts, much of the information can be retained by your audience. Many of the presentations you will give throughout your career will probably be the informative kind. Giving sales reports, running staff meetings, presenting research, analyzing competitive products, training, even meeting with your boss or staff – all can be informative presentations. Are you involved in volunteer work, church or community service? Chances are you will be giving an informative presentation in your outside activities as well. Informative speeches are more than just facts and figures. Even a highly technical presentation which must have many facts and figures can be made more interesting to the appropriate audience.

If you have ever listened to a politician trying to get votes, you've listened to a **Persuasive Speech**. A persuasive speech is used to generate action or influence an audience. It can use logic as well as feelings and emotions to appeal to the audience. Successful business speakers use these tactics as well to enhance their credibility with the audience. Throughout your life, you will probably find yourself in situations where knowing how to give an effective persuasive presentation will serve you well. Some of these situations may include:

- persuading a prospective client to choose your company
- persuading your employees to work longer hours
- persuading management to fund a project
- persuading your boss to promote you or give you a raise
- persuading voters to vote for you
- persuading a valuable potential employee to join your firm
- persuading your school board to grant funding

You may not give many formal persuasive presentations, but you will certainly find yourself in situations where it is essential to deliver a persuasive presentation in an effective way.

The third type of speech can be to **Entertain.** No, I don't mean stand-up comedy or a motivational seminar. But, you may, at some point in your career or in your personal life, find yourself in situations being asked to give a presentation that falls into this category. This can include everything from a welcome speech to a eulogy. It can be part of a retirement dinner, birthday luncheon, sports banquet, award ceremony or a wedding toast. These presentations are commonplace for some speakers, and rare events for others. When you are asked to give a speech for entertainment purposes, be very clear in establishing what the specific purpose of your speech will be, and who else will be presenting. You don't want to find yourself at a retirement dinner giving almost the same speech as the person who speaks before you.

Now that you have established the type of speech you will be giving, it's time to move on to another crucial pre-speech detail. Who are you going to be speaking to?

The "A" in PAL™ refers to your audience

Who are they, and what are they expecting to hear from you? The time it takes you to prepare an audience profile may mean the difference between success and failure for your presentation. Just imagine the chagrin a presenter could feel if she begins her speech on the benefits of a new method of childbirth to a room full of senior citizens. If the audience isn't interested in your topic, there is little you can do to make your presentation work. If you are speaking about Medicare reform to recent college graduates about to face the job market for the first time, your audience will be less than captive. If, on the other hand, you will be speaking to fellow accountants, attorneys or teachers, you already have a great deal of information that will make it easier to create your presentation. If you are speaking within your company or industry, you will probably be able to judge whether or not an audience will be hostile or receptive, depending on the topic. If it's bonuses, you're in luck. If it's downsizing, you may have a difficult time. When you are able to choose a topic yourself, knowing who comprises the audience will let you select a subject that interests as many members as possible. The best source for information about your audience will be the program organizer. You can also ask people you know, or get in touch with those who have addressed the same group before. Misjudging your audience or not knowing who the members are can have disastrous effects on even the best-executed presentation. Sometimes the program organizer has his or her own agenda. Also, talk to people who will be in the audience. You can check out the Internet, get annual reports or promotional materials to help you learn more about the group. Read literature about the company and any information pertaining to its corporate culture. Knowing who you are speaking to will help put you in control.

How to develop an audience profile

What do you want to know and need to know about your audience members before beginning to create your presentation? Who they are, where they are from, what their positions are (in their industries, companies), and what they might think about your topic are all important. Try to uncover their attitudes toward you and your subject. Who are the decision makers and influencers, and what motivates them? What are their concerns or experiences with the subject you will be talking about? When developing your own audience profile, include the following categories: demographics, psychographics, attitudes, learning styles and identification of the decision makers.

Demographics:
What do you know about your audience?

Demographics include audience characteristics such as age, education, occupation, socioeconomic group and marital status, and will affect the way you use language, the information you choose to include, illustrations and examples, and humor if you are including any.

The more details you have about your audience the less risk there is of offending anyone and including too much or too little information. You need to know who will be represented in your audience. Will officers of the company be there? Will there be many departments with their own agendas, or will you be speaking to a narrower base? Will you be speaking to employees at your own level, or from different levels? The wider the range in your audience, the more difficult it is to tailor your presentation to meet everyone's needs. If you will be speaking in something other than a business situation, it becomes even more difficult to analyze the audience members. Are they all residents of the same town? Do they all attend the same church or synagogue? Are they all the parents of teenagers? Establishing a common bond with your audience members will be easier once you know more about them.

Demographic audience profile
When developing an audience profile, include the

following demographics:

- Male/female and percentage of each
- Age range
- Income levels
- Race
- Religion
- Introvert/extrovert
- Business/technical
- Education levels
- Where do they live?
- Where do they work?
- Marital status

Psychographics:
What traits do they share?

Identifying your audience's psychographics is the next step. These traits will help you to further develop your audience profile based upon what you can learn about their feelings and impressions of you and your topic.

Psychographic audience profile

A psychographic profile should include the following audience data:

- What do they think about your topic? Is it new to them?
- Have they attended any presentations on similar topics?
- What are their hopes, aspirations, dreams, goals?
- What are their interests?

- Why are they attending the presentation?
- Do they want to be there?
- Are they politically active?
- Have they supported causes like yours before?
- Are they open-minded?

Identifying decision makers

Is the company president going to be there, your immediate supervisor, or someone you are trying to influence? Knowing in advance if decision makers will be in the audience will help you target your remarks. It will also let you know who the audience will be looking to for feedback and impressions. Capturing a positive reaction from decision makers in attendance can make your presentation a success even if others in the audience disagree. If you have identified a decision maker in the audience, avoid a common pitfall — addressing your comments to this person or looking primarily at him or her during the presentation. This could backfire by making the rest of the audience feel less important.

WIIFM: What's in it for me?

Each member of your audience comes to a presentation with an agenda of his or her own, and wants something from you, the speaker. What these audience members will be looking for may be revealed with answers to the following questions:

- What have their experiences (with the topic) been?
- Why are they there? Do they want to be/have to be?
- What do they hope to get out of the presentation?

- What are their important issues?
- Are they there with an open mind?
- What do they expect from you?

"L" is for Logistics

Why are logistics important? Have you ever had a long lunch immediately followed by a slide presentation in a darkened room? That's a sure combination for an audience dozing if not outright sleeping. A well-prepared speaker takes time in advance to find out details that can ease tension on the actual speech day. For example, if the speaker at the presentation following that long lunch kept the room bright, used more interactive visual aids, and kept the topic moving quickly, the chance of having post-lunch nappers would have been greatly reduced, if not eliminated.

When determining logistics, find out the following:

- What time will you be presenting?
- Who speaks before you? After you?
- How much time will each speaker have?
- What happens if speakers run over their allotted time limits?
- How long will there be for questions and answers?
- Will the Q & A be held at the end of each speaker's portion, or will they be at the very end?
- Where will you be presenting? What is the size of the room and how will it be set up?
- What equipment is available? Will a microphone be provided or must you bring your own?

- What is the exact location of the presentation, its correct address, room, floor, and exact directions to the site?

You will also need to know how many people will be in the audience so that you have the appropriate number of handouts and use the correct visuals for that size group.

When you get to the site, find out where the rest rooms are so you won't be wandering around looking for them during the program breaks.

Collecting & using your information

Collecting information to support your ideas will take the most time in the preparation process. Once your PAL™ has been clearly defined, you already have your first step completed. Now you will write your central theme – one sentence which defines your objective. Use a verb – to inform about, to get commitment for, etc. The theme is what you want to achieve as a result of the presentation. It must be clearly defined and doable. Once the central theme is written, your next step is to collect information. Since you are the expert, start to gather information by using what you already know. Brainstorm and write down key words and phrases about your subject. I use a large wall filled with different-colored note cards to create my speeches. This allows me to move information around as I am outlining my presentation.

After outlining what you do know about the topic, move on to using outside data and research. All information should be current, relevant and correct. Using other people's theories and presenting them as facts can get you in trouble and cause your audience to question your credibility.

Facts and statistics alone often become data dumps, not the most interesting or memorable way to give information.

You can use facts and statistics to support and validate your own ideas. For example, if you are speaking about the value of hiring consultants instead of full-time employees, you can use researched evidence to back up your claims showing reduced costs of employee benefits, lack of paid vacations, and other company cost savings, for example. If you are trying to convince a group to take action, use statistics to illustrate what previously happened to those who took (or didn't take) a similar action. For example, if you are trying to get your neighbors to support a community watch program, show statistics which demonstrate the reduction in crime for city blocks with community patrolling vs. streets without patrols.

Using examples and stories can help reinforce the points you want to make to your audience. Relating personal anecdotes is not only entertaining, but allows your audience to visualize a situation where something happened. For example, if your topic is stricter controls in airline baggage handling, you might use your own trials and tribulations as a business traveler waiting for checked sample cases only to receive them opened and with missing items.

Visualizations are also helpful. To illustrate misleading packaging, you might show two cans of tuna, both exactly the same size, but with differing weights. By reading the labels and showing the cans to the audience, they will be able to see as well as hear your point. And it also makes your presentation more memorable.

What types of outside data work best? Using information other than what you know should enhance and add color to your presentation. If you are preparing a persuasive presentation, now is the time to bring in the experts to support your theories. Who else thinks like you do and has credibility? Has a nationally recognized expert been quoted saying something to support your ideas? Have respected journals published statistics to back you up? If you can demonstrate to audience members the logic of your position, and back it up with the opinions of experts, it will help them to better understand your position.

You can use outside data within your presentation in various ways. Examples, stories, quotations, comparisons and contrasts, statistics and visual aids can all make your presentation come to life for the audience. Which ones to use will depend on your topic. For example:

- Using examples can illustrate your point but not validate it. Use facts and figures for validation.
- Quotations give you the chance to add an expert's opinion to back up your own, or they can be used as attention-getters.

- Comparisons provide similarities, contrasts provide differences. Use them to help audience members relate what they already know to what you want them to know.
- Statistics are useful to support your own theories or disprove others.
- Visual aids help audiences to understand your information, visualize places or things they might not know of, and can be used to bring statistics to life.
- Stories add entertainment for the audience. Share your stories but keep them relevant to the topic and not overly long.
- Appropriate humor can add a light touch, and laughing is a proven way to relax an audience.

While humor can be incorporated into your presentation, it's important to remember some guidelines when using humorous examples and anecdotes.

Some guidelines to consider before using humor:

- If humor does not come naturally to you, don't use it until you are comfortable doing so. Practice at least three to six times, and if it still doesn't come out comfortably, leave it out of your presentation.
- If you are not comfortable with long stories, use one-liners.
- If you're not sure something is funny, try it out on a friend, spouse or co-worker. If in doubt, leave it out.
- Try to surprise your audience with your humor; don't start off by saying, "I want to share this funny story with you." It's better to surprise them with it.
- If no one laughs, try to say something to ease the

silence, for example: "That's the last time I ask my attorney if something is funny."

- Don't laugh too hard at your own jokes. It's OK to let your enthusiasm for the anecdote show, but laughing too hard is in poor taste.

If you choose to use humor:

You can use humor successfully if you stick to the guidelines. First, make sure it's appropriate for the occasion. Unless it specifically pertains to your company, you're sure everyone there will understand it, and no one will be offended, proceed with caution. Inside company jokes can be very funny. But only if everyone gets the joke. When used properly, humor can be a wonderful icebreaker. In a room where few know each other, it can make friends out of strangers and sympathetic listeners out of apathetic ones. Stories about yourself are safest; everyone enjoys a good joke at someone else's expense – when it's done with good taste and the joke is told by you, about you.

If you have decided to use humor, here are six guidelines to help you:

1. **Remember the punch line.** A great story isn't so great if you can't remember the end. It will also lose credibility for you with the audience.
2. **The anecdote should relate to your speech and be appropriate.** Don't speak about your children's exploits when the group includes infertile couples.
3. **Have good timing.** Practice your anecdote. Tell it to several people and watch their reactions. If the story doesn't go over well, modify or eliminate it. Practice

until you feel comfortable with the material.

4. Don't be cruel. You might think fat jokes are funny, but it's likely that someone in the audience has had a weight problem or is sympathetic to someone who does.

5. Don't use vulgar language. Even if your audience is a room full of "the guys," it's never appropriate.

6. Humor doesn't travel and it doesn't work overseas. This is even true regionally within the United States. Always keep your audience in mind. What's funny in New York may not be funny in Memphis.

Remembering humorous anecdotes may seem easy when you first hear them or think of them but chances are, just like anything else, you'll forget the whole story if you wait to write it down. Save yourself some grief and write the story down as soon as you think of it or hear it. Then when it's time to prepare your presentation, you'll have a collection of humorous anecdotes ready to use.

Part Three

What You Need To Know About Using Visual Aids

"People who keep it simple the longest are the most successful."
— **Kirk McCaskill,** Chicago White Sox

Our ability to retain information increases by almost 40 percent when visual aids are used. As a presenter, that means you have a greater opportunity to make an impact on your audience. Proper use of visual aids allows complicated information to be broken down into parts, making it easier for audience comprehension. The speaker also benefits, allowing you to move during your presentation and help the audience stay focused.

Five rules to remember when using visual aids

1. Visual aids should be simple enough for the audience to understand the concept in less than 20 seconds. If the material is complex, do a gradual build — start with an easy-to-understand point and work up to the more complex.

2. Leave the visual aid up long enough for your audience to look it over before you begin talking about it.

3. Don't make visuals so complicated that the audience has to keep reading while you are talking.

4. Don't talk to the screen, talk to the audience. Stand so that the visual aid is to your left. Point with your left hand, which should be closest to the screen when you begin to speak. We read from left to right, so we want to point to the beginning of the sentence.

5. Practice with the visual aids before your presentation so that you are comfortable working with them and your equipment.

6. If something goes wrong with the visual aids or equipment, keep going. Turn the machine off, if necessary, and proceed without any visual aids. Remember: The visuals are an aid for the audience, not you, so be able to present without them. Always come prepared with back-up bulbs, extension cords and anything else that could malfunction.

Choosing a visual aid

Today's technology offers you a wide option of visual aids to add to the more traditional modes like slides, overheads and flip charts. Different presentations will require different kinds of visuals. For a simple staff meeting, a flip chart can work well. For a more elaborate sales presentation, one of the newer computer-driven action shows might be appropriate. To determine which method works best for you, practice using a few different types before you make a final decision. You may wish to use more than one type of visual aid during your presentation, for example: flip charts and overheads or slides and videos. You may find that the type of visual aid you choose depends upon several variables:

- the length of your presentation
- the audience size
- the logistics of the meeting room
- the available equipment
- the type of presentation you will be giving

Don't get so comfortable using one type of visual aid that you are reluctant to try anything else. Even a presentation that you may have given 50 times can take on new life by changing the type of visual aids.

Types of visual aids & how to use them

Flip charts

A flip chart is a large pad of paper mounted on an easel. It is bound at the top and loose at the bottom. (There are now electronic flip charts. A camera captures the image, then it gets printed). As you fill up one page (using a marker), flip it over and start another. Flip charts are best used in small, informal groups. You can write as you speak, or put your points on the flip chart in advance of the meeting. You can add points as your meeting progresses. A flip chart can look sloppy by the end of your presentation, and it can be hard to go back to a previous point unless you tear off the pages and post them around the room. When writing on a flip chart use large letters (2 to 4 inches high); blue or black markers are easiest to read. Never use red and green together. Many people are colorblind and cannot see these colors. They will not be able to differentiate your points. Follow the 4 x 4 rule: use no more than four lines, and four words per line, on any flip chart page. Write only on the top three-fourths of the page. Some presenters write their points very lightly in pencil, in advance of presentations. Then, during the presentation, they are able to write over their points with marker. If you have written very faintly, the audience may not even notice the penciled notes. This is also good for diagrams and graphs. When presenting from flip charts, be sure to stand on the correct side. If you are right-handed, the flip chart should be to your left. When you begin to write, move slightly to the left and you will be in the correct position. Left-handed presenters should do the reverse. Remember the three T's — **touch, turn** and **talk** – as you use your visual aids. You are speaking to the audience, not to the flip chart. After you touch your key point, turn to the audience, establish eye contact with someone, and continue to talk. Use the hand closest to the flip chart when touching it. If possible, use pushpins to attach the finished pages to the walls so the audience can see what has already been discussed. You will also be able to add things if needed.

Overhead projection

Even with the amount of new technologies available today, the overhead projector is still widely used. Nearly every conference room or meeting site has one, and many presenters have their own. There are many different types of overhead projectors, including small, inexpensive, portable ones that are easy to transport.

Beware: Poor quality overheads will detract from, not enhance, your presentation. To use an overhead projection system, you will need the following: a projector (with a working bulb), clear plastic sheets called transparencies, and markers or grease pencils. Place the transparencies one at a time on the glass surface of the projector. They are illuminated by the bulb, and a lens projects the image onto a screen or blank wall. Professional-looking transparencies should be made well in advance of your presentation. You can make them yourself using a computer and printer. Use 18- to 22-point bold typeface. The projected images can be large enough to be seen by a large group or small enough for meetings held in conference rooms. Purchase frames made to hold the transparencies, which make them easier to handle. The frames also protect the transparencies and can be stored in a binder. Number your transparencies and place them in order before your presentation. Mark the order on your speech outline.

Warning: Overheads are often used excessively. Many people put their whole presentations on transparencies, forcing the audience to read and watch the screen instead of the speaker. Transparencies should be used to enhance the key points of your presentation, not serve as a substitute for it. You don't want audience members reading when they should be listening.

When presenting, do not stand at the overhead projector. You will end up blocking some portion of the audience unless the screen is above your head. The other disadvantage of standing at the projector is that you will tend to look down at the visual rather than at the audience. Stand to the side of the screen and use your left hand or a pointer. Touch, turn to the audience, and talk. If you are not using the pointer, put it away. Only use it to point at the screen, and never point it at your audience.

When presenting with overheads, make sure you arrive early enough to turn on the machine and make any necessary adjustments. Check the neck to make sure it projects high enough onto the screen so your audience can see the transparencies. Carry an extension cord in case you want to move the machine, and an extra light bulb in case one burns out. Make sure you know how to replace the bulb in advance. During your presentation, turn off the machine for periods of time. This allows you to move around and connect with listeners. When you turn the machine on again, it becomes more interesting for the audience. I use an intermittent on/off connector from Radio Shack. I can hold the clicker in my hand (like a remote mouse) and turn the machine on and off without standing next to it. Audiences love it!

Slides

Slides are still widely used, especially for scientific presentations. They can be easily designed on your computer and work well for large group presentations. The best slides have dark backgrounds and light typeface. This allows you to keep a few or all of the lights on during your presentation. When you turn off all of the lights, people get sleepy. Limit the number of slides you use and keep the wording brief. Use blank slides to turn the audience's attention back to you. Pie charts and simple graphs work well as slides. Use several colors to differentiate your points.

When presenting with slides, stand at the front of the room and face your audience. Use a remote control to change the slides. If you have trouble differentiating between the forward and reverse buttons, put a piece of tape on one of them so you will be able to distinguish them by touch. Before your presentation, make sure you have checked that all of your slides are in correct order and position. An upside-down slide or one that is from another presentation will make you look ill-prepared. Here, too, it's a good idea to carry an extension cord and extra bulb, just in case. When you finish with the visual aid, turn the projector off and raise the lights if they were dimmed.

Handouts

Handouts are typed pages pertaining to your presentation and contain information you want the audience to have. They can have copies of charts, slides or graphs or other visual aids as well. Handouts can be an outline of your key points, or contain information you have chosen not to include in your presentation. They should be neat, well-presented and have your name, address and telephone number on them (if you would like your audience to be able to contact you). They can also contain biographical information about you and may give some background facts about your company or service. The purpose of handouts is to enhance your speech, not detract from it, so make sure they are clear and easy to read.

Use handouts when:

- your speech contains a lot of technical information
- you can't put all the information in your speech
- you want your audience to have the option of taking notes
- you want added value for your audience to take away

Make sure to tell the audience what information is available in the handout, so they can decide when, or if, to take copious notes. If you don't want them to read the handouts during your presentation, don't give them out until the end.

Video systems

Video systems can be used for a variety of purposes: playback of prerecorded tapes, computer-controlled presentations using video monitors or projectors, live video of remote events, and recording and playing during a presentation. Because video systems usually involve several pieces of equipment, planning, prechecking and rechecking are essential. Keep in mind that if you are not bringing your own equipment with you, video playback systems vary. Make sure the format of the tape you are using is compatible with the playback machine at the presentation site. Check the compatibility before attempting to play any tapes. An on-site inspection of the equipment and the room will save you embarrassing problems later on. If you will be recording as well as using playback, make sure you have made your requirements known when requesting the equipment. When I videotape the participants at my seminars, conferences and workshops, I usually bring my own equipment, including two camcorders and my own tripod. I bring two cameras in case one breaks. Since playback equipment is too heavy and cumbersome to transport myself, I arrange for it to be on-site when I arrive. I always arrive early enough to arrange the proper lighting and test all the equipment, so I won't have to spend time making adjustments when the audience is in the room. If I am going to be audio taping, I make certain I have extra extension cords, batteries and tapes. I test the equipment myself before I begin to tape during the presentation.

Video monitors

What size monitor should you use to make sure everyone in the auditorium can see properly? Here are some general guidelines:

Audience size	Monitor size
10 or under	19 inches
11–25	25 inches
26–75	4 to 6 feet

For larger audiences, several large monitors will be needed.

LCD panels & projectors

Liquid Crystal Display (LCD) panels and projectors are

fast replacing slide presentations. LCD panels and projectors enable you to use higher quality visuals in your presentation. Even newer technology is being developed as I write this book.

LCD panels are connected to the video port of a computer, and let you project images on a blank wall or screen. Combined with a laptop computer, they are easy to use and transport. LCD panels are designed for use with overhead projectors. For good quality images, the overhead projector should produce a standard measure of light of no less than 4,000 lumens. The LCD panels themselves are flat devices that are about the thickness of a laptop computer and weigh about 7 pounds. The screens range in size from 8 to 10 inches, and can project images as large as 10 feet. The panels can change screens quickly and produce clearer images and better color reproduction than other methods of projection.

The LCD projectors are self-contained units combining LCD display, a light source and projection. Although they are heavier than LCD panels, you have everything you need in one place. There is no need for an overhead projector. Since the light source is built-in, it can be matched to features of the LCD display, producing higher quality images. This technology is changing rapidly; the weight and cost are decreasing, and resolution is getting better.

Multimedia presentations
No longer exclusively the domain of professionals, you

can create your own multimedia presentations using a computer. There is software available that will allow your computer to display digital video sequences, transport your audience to out-of-sequence slides, or even incorporate other presentations. Multimedia presentation computer packages can include drawing tools for graphics creation, and prescripted buttons that can be set to trigger internal events such as starting a video sequence. If you are going to use an entry-level multimedia presentation package, most of the software available can produce transition effects (wipes, dissolves, etc.) and moving-typeface-style animations that let you sequentially march topics onto the screen. You will also be able to incorporate movies into your slides using programs for either Macintosh® or PC. In addition, some programs have begun to incorporate hypertext-like features that can provide interaction with your presentation. Depending on the needs of your audience, you can alter the content of your presentation on the fly. There are also entry-level programs conceived from the outset to integrate text, graphics, audio, animation and video elements into well-coordinated presentations. Because these software packages are constantly changing, it's best to get as much information as possible before purchasing one.

Computer presentation reminders

- Check your setup and power sources. Bring a pair of screwdrivers along with your computer in case you need to connect cables or peripherals.

- Bring extension cords, power surge protectors and cables you might need.
- Bring duct tape and scissors to secure wires to the floor and walls so no one will trip.
- Be sure your power pack is fully charged or new batteries have been installed.
- Carry an auxiliary light with you or request one if the room will be darkened.
- If you are using a modem, verify that the room has compatible phone jacks and that they work.
- Have duplicate copies of your software with you.
- Run through your presentation using the computer visuals, and make sure they can be seen from all seats.
- Practice using the equipment until you are completely comfortable with it.

Writing for visual aids

When preparing your visual aids, remember that their purpose is to enhance your presentation, not detract from it. What you are going to say is, obviously, the most important aspect, but good visuals will help you capture and hold your audience's attention. When writing your visuals, remember the following points:

Typeface. Choose one that is easy to read. Sans-serif type is ideal for headlines, serif is better for text (sans-serif lacks "feet"). Be consistent and use the same font for all titles, and the same for all text. Don't use more than two fonts. Use 18- to 22-point-size boldface type. **Keep it simple.** Reading too many words will tire your audience. Use words to describe your points and summarize when possible. Save the complicated information for your presentation and handout.

Be consistent. On a single visual, if your bulleted points are in the form of questions, keep them all in question style. If they are in the form of statements, keep them that way.

Titles. Limit the title of a visual to one line and subtitles to two lines. Don't put the title of the program on every visual, they will begin to look cluttered.

Capitalization. Do not capitalize all words. IT'S TOO DIFFICULT TO READ. Use initial capitals for titles. Capitalize any proper names.

Graphs & charts enhance visual aids

Graphs

Simply constructed graphs and charts help an audience grasp your point, make comparisons, or view specific items in relation to the whole. Line graphs make it easy to illustrate trends and show increases or decreases in a quick way. Profile graphs use shading underneath the data and make it easy to see large or significant changes. Bar graphs let your audience see blocks of information, allowing them to quickly make visual comparisons. Pictographs use pictures rather than a line or a bar to show the same type of information.

Charts

Organization charts help to clarify complex subjects or procedures. They are useful to detail social groups or chains of command. They can help your audience quickly see and understand your subject. Pie charts clearly depict pieces in relation to the whole and to one another; it is a way to simplify a combination of details for your audience. Flowcharts show a series of sequences or relationships in an easy-to-follow format.

PROFILE GRAPH

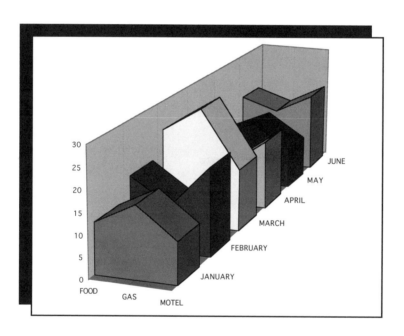

FIGURE BAR GRAPH

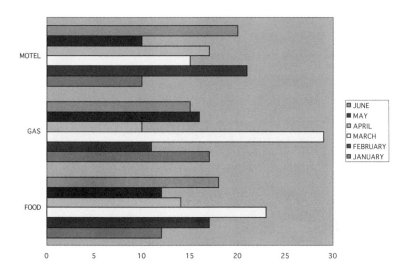

FLOWCHART

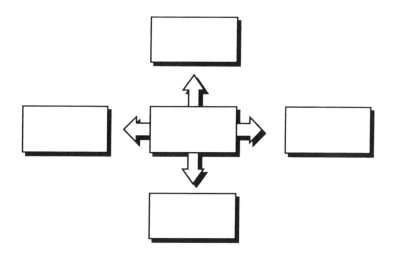

LINE CHART

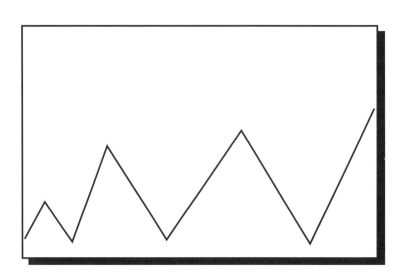

PIE CHART

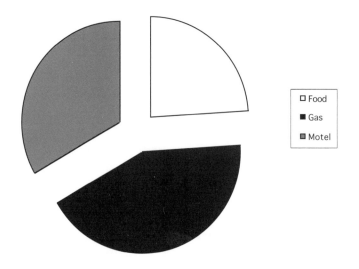

- □ Food
- ■ Gas
- ▣ Motel

ORGANIZATION CHART

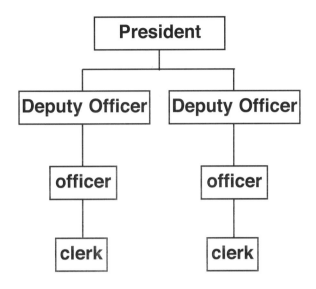

ROOM ARRANGEMENTS

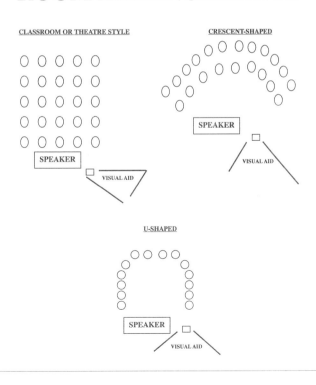

Use visual aids wisely

Visual aids need to be planned, executed and used wisely. Your audience and topic will help you determine which type of visual aid to use. The location of your presentation may dictate the method you choose. Always make sure you have verified the available equipment and power supply before deciding which type of visual aid to use. If possible, have a backup system with you, just in case. Be prepared to give your presentation without visual aids. After all, things go wrong with even the best-prepared events.

Visual aids reminders

- Check the room setup and equipment availability before preparing your visual aids.
- If possible, practice using the visuals on-site.
- Arrive early on the day of your presentation to have adequate time to set up equipment.
- Carry extra bulbs, extension cords, duct tape, scissors and tools.
- If using computers, make sure all electrical outlets are grounded.
- Make sure your power pack is fully charged or new batteries have been installed on your laptop.
- Use a wireless mouse.
- Make sure proper phone jacks are available if you are using a modem.
- Make sure the keyboard operator has an auxiliary light if the room is to be darkened.
- Bring duplicate copies of software.

- If renting or borrowing equipment, make sure you are familiar with it in advance of your presentation.
- Make sure your visuals can be seen from every seat.
- When using slides, make sure they are in order and none are upside down.
- Make sure everything is spelled correctly, especially customers' names and products.
- Be prepared to speak without visuals, just in case!

Part Four

Organizing Your Presentation

"The most important thing is how a guy prepares himself to do battle."
– **Hank Aaron,** professional baseball player & legend

Unlike a paper which people can read at their own pace, and reread when necessary, you have only one chance to be clear in an oral presentation. The method of organization that you choose will be a reflection of the type of speech you will be giving: informative, persuasive or entertaining. Your audience members will depend on you to show them the way to understanding; a well-organized presentation acts as a road map to guide the audience from one point to the next. It should have a well-designed introduction, a body that leads them where you want them to go, and a strong conclusion to tie it all together.

Developing your outline

Develop an outline as a planning tool to give shape and form to your presentation. Regardless of the purpose of your presentation, the outline will help you to develop an effective presentation. The preferred method of outlining is the phrase outline method. Phrases are long enough to remind you of what you want to say, and short enough so your attention will be on the audience and not on the outline. The problem with writing full sentences is that speakers have the tendency to read, word for word, what is on their notes. Keep the language conversational. You will need transitions to prevent gaps between you and your listeners. Transition sentences are used between the review of your main points and your final, memorable statement. Transitions, numbers you need to remember, or other important statements that must be spoken exactly, as is, can be written out. Transitions enable the speakers to repeat ideas without being redundant. They help move the listeners from point to point, and, should they be drifting, transitions reiterate what has just been said. Examples of transitions are: another way to look at; along with; we have just covered; let's move on to the next point; and the second point is.

Organization of the informative speech

The informative speech can effectively be organized in one of six ways:

1. Chronological order. Arranged in order of occurrence or a time sequence. If your topic follows in a progression, you might use a time line to illustrate the process. Visual aids can be effective in demonstrating the time span to your audience. An example is describing the three phases of clinical trials a drug must go through before applying for FDA approval.

Chronological Order
50 Years of Change In Television
Viewing Habits

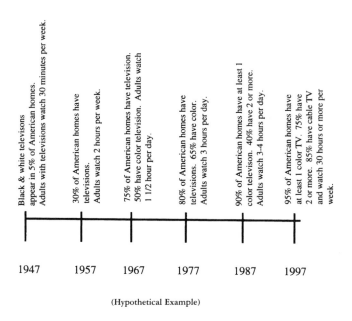

(Hypothetical Example)

2. Spatial order. Since spatially organized presentations pertain to the nature of space, they are most effective when combined with visual aids. If your presentation is about the differences in movie theaters' treatment of patrons in wheelchairs, visuals showing the different layouts of the theaters' would help the audience to visualize the best (and worst) ways to arrange the seating for these patrons.

Example of Spatial Order
Setting Up Classroom Learning Centers

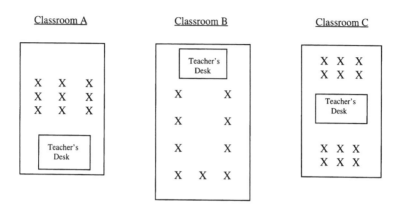

3. **Geographical order.** This presentation is also arranged spatially, but by geographical space. If you are discussing the early colonization of the United States, using visuals of how the states looked in relation to each other during different periods in U.S. history would effectively demonstrate to the audience the different geographical areas involved, their sizes in relation to each other, and changes compared to recent history. This is also effective in describing sales territories or regions.

4. **Topical order.** This type of speech takes a large topic and divides it. Think of the topic of private vs. public schooling today. Private schools could be further divided by parochial, same-sex schools, boarding schools and day schools. Public schools could be broken down by inner city vs. suburban and rural. This method works well for

discussing a variety of products.

5. Comparison and contrast. This presentation compares characteristics, features and qualities that are similar and then contrasts their differences. It helps to clarify the unknown by comparing it to the known. If you are comparing the differences between whole life and term insurance you would point out the cost factors and the savings factors of each type of insurance policy.

6. Cause and effect. The presentation organized by cause and effect has a distinct order. First, what has happened, or what will happen, and then what the results will be. For example, if your company allows job sharing for some employees but not others, you may have disgruntled employees, possibly risk lawsuits, and end with an unproductive work force. You also can give multiple scenarios and conclusions using the cause-and-effect format.

Creating and organizing persuasive presentations

Have you ever ordered anything while watching a TV commercial or infomercial? Did you ever buy a magazine subscription over the telephone or from someone who came to your door? If you answered in the affirmative, then you have responded to a persuasive presentation. How can you be persuasive? By using various methods of proof to convince your audience members to do or think what you want them to. The ancient Greek philosopher Aristotle talked about using **Logos, Pathos**

Speech Planning Worksheet

Type: Persuasive   Organizational Style: Standard

CENTRAL THEME:

Consider: Purpose, Audience, and Logistics (PAL)

Main Point

Supporting Information/Data:

Transition:

Main Point

Supporting Information/Data:

Transition:

Main Point

Supporting Information/Data:

Transition:

Introduction 10 - 15%

Grabber:

Source Credibility:

WIIFT:

Preview:

Conclusion 5 - 10%

Review:

Memorable Statement/Call-To-Action:

43

and **Ethos** as methods of persuasion, and they are just as valid today.

Logos in Greek means reason, and is how the word logic is derived. It contains your facts and figures, statistics and other forms of documentation. This type of information can be slanted to support the presenter's own philosophy. Just listen to any politician at election time. With the same campaign issues, one politician will try to convince you that the only way to improve things is to raise taxes. His or her opponent will try to persuade you that the only way to improve things is to lower taxes. Now the lower tax position may be the one most people will go for right up front, but a successful politician can persuade voters that increased taxes is a good thing! Logos also includes a logical progression of ideas.

Pathos, also from the Greek, refers to using emotions. This is the method for appealing to the needs, wants and desires of your audience members. Most decisions are made using a combination of logic and emotion (logos and pathos). Understanding the needs of your audience members is vital to persuading them. You want them to feel good about their decisions, and can combine logos and pathos to do this. While many scientific thinkers claim to use only logic to make decisions, we are more subtly influenced by emotion than we may care to admit.

The third mode of proof is ethos, or credibility. How are you perceived by your audience? What are your credentials, and are you a credible speaker for the topic? Many people vote strictly along party lines regardless of who is the candidate. Their party's candidates are perceived as being the best for the job strictly because of party affiliation. Credibility is not an issue for the individual candidate, only for his or her party. If the party loses face, the candidates will suffer as well. Since decisions were made strictly by ethos, the candidate's individuality didn't matter.

What are the major components of credibility? Credibility consists of three components: perceived trustworthiness, perceived competence, and perceived conviction. Regardless of whether or not the presenter is actually any of these things, the audience's perception is what matters. If the audience perceives the presenter as being trustworthy, competent and having the power of his or her convictions, that is what is important. It is then up to the speaker to confirm what the audience believes. If, however, credibility is an issue, how do you deal with it? Your competency can be established by an introduction that states your credentials and accomplishments. The force of your convictions will be established during your presentation as you demonstrate your knowledge and display your convictions. Your trustworthiness, however, is more difficult to establish. A classic approach to establishing trust is through common ground. It involves sharing the similarities between you and your audience – demographics, attitudes, experiences all count toward establishing trust. For example: "I've lived in Philadelphia for the past 25 years, as have many of you. I am a product of Philadelphia public schools, as are many of you. I've been paying Philadelphia city taxes for the past 25 years, as have many of you. I want to pay less – as do many of you." You have established common ground – where you live, where you went to school, taxes, dissatisfaction with the taxes you pay. All these common bonds count toward establishing trust with your audience.

Most successful presentations have some elements of all three modes of persuasion. The speaker's style and analysis of the audience and topic help him or her decide how much of each to use. In addition to having three possible modes of persuasion, persuasive presentations also have three levels of persuasion: to motivate, to convince, and to call to action.

Motivation is the first level of persuasion. You want to excite members of your audience about what is being shared with them, but you probably won't be altering their opinions or beliefs. Motivation can be as familiar as a church sermon or a speech by the coach of a sports team getting his players fired up before their game. You want your audience members to feel good about what you are telling them and about themselves. All presentations should be motivational.

The second level of persuasion is to **convince**. You want your audience to change its opinions or to develop the same opinion as yours. You may not want them to do anything but change their minds. If they haven't yet formed an opinion, you want them to adopt yours. For example, if your company does not offer on-site day care, and you believe it will benefit both employees and the employers if they open a day-care facility, you want your audience to share your opinions.

Then you move on to the third level of persuasion, **a call to action.** You want the audience to do something, in the case of day care, to join with you to convince management that on-site day care is essential for the company to provide. This is the most difficult level of persuasion to achieve. Any persuasive presentation can be prepared using the same method. Developing an outline will be the first step. Following the format provided here, first state your purpose: motivate, convince or call to action. You may want to do a combination of two – convince and call to action. Be clear about your objectives. You will ultimately use your purpose to determine the effectiveness of the presentation. Next, identify your audience and the attitudes you will be facing: favorable, hostile, apathetic, uninformed or a combination: favorable mix or hostile mix. In order for your presentation to be effective, you need to have an understanding of who you will be speaking to and something about their mind-set. When determining this attitude, keep the following six audience types in mind:

Favorable audience: They already share your opinions and probably want what you want. For example: other employees who are currently paying for off-site day care and for whom it is stressful both to pay for it and keep work hours that match the day care's hours.

Hostile audience: First, understand why the audience is hostile: is it your topic, request, philosophy, or are they just a hard group to win over? For example: I once traveled across the country to give a seminar on business etiquette in a corporate setting to middle managers in a large corporation. When I entered the meeting room and went to introduce myself, no one greeted me. I wanted to diffuse the situation right away, so instead of opening the session by talking about what I hoped to cover in the seminar, I began by asking them why they objected to the topic.

Now they knew I would be listening to them and they began to open up and talk about their feelings and why they felt hostile. One of the things they objected to was why upper management thought they needed etiquette training, and wasn't it common sense anyway? When I explained that upper management had already taken this same program and that there was much more to business etiquette than common sense they began to respond to me in a positive way. They knew that I was listening to them and dealing with their objections. On another occasion I was asked to facilitate a program that was being rolled out to a sales department who thought it was a waste of time. Their feelings were obviously negative, so I opened by asking them why they were against the program. After listening to why they didn't think they needed the training, I was able to turn things around by telling them about improvements that came from the program. I then was able to ask them about areas where they could improve their skills, and they began to see that I was interested in helping them. I demonstrated that I understood their concerns and was there to work with them.

Apathetic audience: They really don't care about what you have to say, and must be made to realize how they will benefit before responding favorably. For example, people in your company without young children probably won't care whether or not there is on-site day care, but by using examples of how they will benefit from it (e.g. less time for co-workers to be late, absent, or have to leave early to meet day-care schedules), on-site day care is a worthwhile project for them to support.

Uninformed audience: They are not opposed to what you have to say, they just don't know anything about it. This audience takes more time to develop, but your goal is clear. Your job is to educate them. For example, if you want me to support on-site day care, you have to demonstrate the benefits for me and for the company. Maybe as a supervisor I won't have to cover for employees who are late or absent because of child-care problems and asking workers to stay late will be easier when they know they can see their children and even have meals with them before returning to work. The company benefits and the supervisors and employees benefit.

Mixed audience: There are two types of mixed audiences: the favorable mix and the hostile mix. The favorable mix includes favorable, uninformed and apathetic members. You will have to inform the uninformed and

convince the apathetic that there is a real need or benefit. If there is even one hostile member of the audience,
the entire audience can shift and align themselves with
the hostile member, and, if so, this group is identified as
a hostile mix. Your audience analysis should have prepared you for the hostile mix and your challenge is to
disarm the hostile members and win them over as soon
as possible. Sometimes the real audience isn't even in
the room. The ultimate decision makers may be hostile,
and the group at hand will need to persuade them. If
you are prepared for a hostile audience, you will be
ready for any mixed group. The hostile mix is probably
the most difficult audience to work with. Organize your
presentation to bring up comments like "If we go with
on-site day care, what are the benefits to your department?" If hostile-mix audience members believe that
you are receptive to their concerns and not afraid to talk
about them, they will be more apt to listen to your
points later on. It is up to you to determine and address
the reasons for hostility. It probably has nothing to do
with you personally. There may be budget cuts, unfair
promotions or other grievances that have nothing to do
with what you want to talk about. A good listener will
gain the respect of the audience. If you are presenting
information that you know will be received negatively,
bury the negatives in the middle of your presentation
and end with the positives. Don't be evasive, you will be
found out sooner or later.

After determining your purpose and audience, think
about the logistics of your presentation. How long will

you have to present? What time of day? Are you part of a group? How large is the audience? Where will you fit in? Then, collect your information. Make sure this information is pertinent, current, accurate, relevant and appropriate. For example, if you will be speaking about on-site day care in your company, make sure you have the facts and can support them with evidence. If you are appealing to your audience members for support, and sense hostility because they don't have any children or perhaps their children are already out of school, you will have to find the "hot buttons" and appeal to them on that level. Perhaps you have research that proves on-site day care improves the productivity of employees who use the service and other employees as well by helping to alleviate tension in their departments. You will be able to relate this information, meet the audience needs, and keep your own agenda at the same time. When you are preparing your data, keep the audience and their needs in mind at all times.

Organizing the persuasive presentation

A persuasive presentation can be organized using one of four methods: **proposition to proof, problem to solution, reflective,** or **motivated sequence.**

Proposition to proof. In this method, your proposition is stated at the beginning of your presentation. Your audience knows right up front what you want from them. Then, you prove your proposition using three to five points of evidence and emotional appeal. Finally, you review the evidence and end with a strong closing statement. Since you want your audience members to be receptive to what you are going to say, you don't want to offend them in the beginning of your presentation. To make people want to change their point of view, give them new information presented in a way they will be able to easily understand. This method works well with favorable audiences, and is possible with some work for uninformed, apathetic and favorable-mixed groups, but is not a good choice for a hostile or hostile-mix audience.

Example of a proposition to proof situation:

Proposition: "I recommend our corporation fund and operate an on-site day-care facility."

Proof:
1. With their children on-site, employees won't feel stressed by rushing to get to work on time or having to leave early to pick up children.
2. Since on-site day care can be either fully or partially funded by the corporation, this is a strong incentive for employees to stay with the corporation.
3. Other corporations with on-site day care have reported only favorable results and cost savings due to less employee absenteeism.

Conclusion: On-site day care offers real benefits for both the corporation and the employees.

Speech Planning Worksheet

Type: Persuasive   Organizational Style: Proposition to Proof

CENTRAL THEME:

Consider: Purpose, Audience, and Logistics (PAL)

PROPOSITION:

Proof:

Introduction 10 - 15%

Grabber:

Source Credibility (optional):

WIIFT:

Preview (optional):

Conclusion 5 - 10%

Review:

Memorable Statement/Call-To-Action:

© Brody Communications Ltd.

P.O. Box 8868 • Elkins Park, PA • 19027 (215) 886-1688 • (800) 726-7936 • Fax (215) 886-1699

Problem to solution. In the problem to solution method, you state the problem and then present a solution from your point of view. The audience must believe that there is a problem, and agree that it must be solved. This must be done before getting to the solution. If the problem is complex, make sure you spend enough time detailing what the problem is. After you have explained the problem clearly, offer your solution, being sure to include three to five points and supporting material, a review, and a memorable closing statement. This works for the same types of audiences as proposition to proof.

Example of a problem to solution situation:

Problem: The turnover rate at your company amongst men and women with young children is far above the national average. What can the company do to reverse this trend?

Your solution: By offering on-site day care partially funded by the company, the company becomes a more desirable place to work. Because many parents of young children have to take days off from work when their child-care arrangement isn't working, having an on-site facility will eliminate this problem. It has also been shown that employees who are able to bring their children to work, see them during the day and spend time commuting with them, are more likely to stay with their current employer for five years or more. I recommend we offer subsidized on-site day care.

Speech Planning Worksheet

Type: Persuasive   Organizational Style: Problem to Solution

CENTRAL THEME:

Consider: Purpose, Audience, and Logistics (PAL)

Problem Definition:

Proposed Solution:

Reason(s) for Proposed Solution:

Introduction 10 - 15%	
Grabber:	**Source Credibility (optional):**
WIIFT:	**Preview (optional):**

Conclusion 5 - 10%
Review:
Memorable Statement/Call-To-Action:

P.O. Box 8868 • Elkins Park, PA • 19027 (215) 886-1688 • (800) 726-7936 • Fax (215) 886-1699

55

Reflective. Using this method, a problem is stated at the beginning of the presentation, the same way as with the problem to solution method. This works most effectively if the speaker and audience agree on a criteria to evaluate each of the possible solutions and to ultimately make a decision. After the problem and the criteria are agreed upon, the solutions are offered and evaluated against the criteria. Effective speakers often present the positive points of each solution, then smash them with evidence to the contrary using the agreed-upon criteria as a basis of evaluation, and finally present the best solution supporting it with plenty of evidence. The solution you like can mention the negatives first and then build up the positives against the criteria. If you are not strong when presenting your beliefs, you will not be able to convince others that your way is the best. Leave no loopholes; make sure that you have eliminated other points of view as viable, leaving your solution as the best choice. This is an excellent approach for analytical people who love to evaluate all details. It can be overkill for favorable, uninformed and apathetic audiences if they are not detail-oriented. This approach can work well with hostile and hostile-mixed groups.

Example of a reflective situation:

This starts exactly the same as problem to solution.

Problem: The turnover rate at your company among both men and women with young children is far above the national average. What can the company do to reverse this trend?

Before coming up with possible solutions, let's agree on the criteria to evaluate these solutions. I think that cost, liability and convenience are important factors. Do you agree? Are there others you would like to add? One solution is: Do nothing. This is the easiest thing to do, however, it won't solve the problem, and the turnover rate is critical. Besides, we are having trouble attracting new hires. Another solution is: Pay for off-site day care. The liability criteria is met but it may be inconvenient. A third option is: Build an on-site day-care facility. The liability will be an issue, one that our attorney says can be overcome, and it is a small concern given the convenience and economic benefit it gives our employees. I recommend that we build an on-site day-care facility to reduce the turnover rate and help us attract quality workers.

Motivated sequence. The motivated sequence is a technique well established in the sales profession. You lead audience members to the brink of action, and then provide them with the means to act. You will either create a need in audience members or make them aware of a need they already have but may not have recognized. You then are able to supply the means to satisfy that need. Your challenge is to make the solution appealing to your audience. For example, a computer software company might approach a client with information demonstrating how another company with similar products was able to increase sales and improve customer satisfaction by installing their customized database. Once the client shows interest and excitement in the product, the salesperson is ready to show how a customized database could increase this client's

Speech Planning Worksheet

Type: Persuasive   Organizational Style: Reflective

CENTRAL THEME:

Consider: Purpose, Audience, and Logistics (PAL)

PROBLEM DEFINITION:

CRITERIA FOR JUDGING POSSIBLE SOLUTIONS:

Possible Solution:

Positives:

Negatives:

Possible Solution:

Negatives:

Positives:

Possible Solution: (presenter's choice)

Positives:

Negatives:

Introduction 10 - 15%

Grabber:

Source Credibility (optional):

WIIFT:

Preview (optional):

Conclusion 5 - 10%

Review:

Memorable Statement/Call-To-Action:

© Brody Communications Ltd.   P.O. Box 8868 • Elkins Park, PA • 19027 (215) 886-1688 • (800) 726-7936 • Fax (215) 886-1699

business, and a sale is probably imminent. It is important to note that explaining the features of a product is not as effective as demonstrating how that product will benefit your client. If there are drawbacks or limitations to what your product can do, bring them up in the middle of your presentation, take the time to refute them, and then move forward with the positives.

Example of a motivated sequence situation:

Get attention: Are you holding yourself back in your career because of your inability to present your ideas?
Create need: In order to become an effective salesperson, you must be an effective presenter. Studies show... .
Satisfaction: If you take a Brody Communications Ltd. seminar you will learn how to:

Organize your ideas
- Read your audience
- Control your stage fright
- Move and use visual aids
- Handle questions comfortably

Visualization: With these skills, you will be able to connect with your audience and sell your ideas. Picture yourself as a regional sales manager... .
Call to action: Telephone, fax, e-mail or visit our Web site at: Brody Communications Ltd. at: **http://www.brodycomm.com**

Knowing how to present persuasively is critical to career development, and will benefit you in other areas of your life as well. The ability to influence others'

Speech Planning Worksheet

Type: Persuasive   Organizational Style: Motivated Sequence

CENTRAL THEME:

Consider: Purpose, Audience, and Logistics (PAL)

Need (problem):

Satisfaction (features):

Visualization (benefits):

Introduction 10 - 15%	
Attention (grabber):	**Source Credibility (optional):**
WIIFT:	**Preview (optional):**

Conclusion 5 - 10%

Review:

Memorable Statement/Call-To-Action:

© Brody Communications Ltd.   P.O. Box 8868 • Elkins Park, PA • 19027 (215) 886-1688 • (800) 726-7936 • Fax (215) 886-1699

beliefs and motivate change is a powerful tool that will enhance your career.

Four models of persuasive speaking

Proposition to Proof:

- Grabber statement.
- State your proposition.
- Proof – Using logic and emotional appeals.
- Review – Draw conclusions.
- Memorable statement – Ask for what you want.

Problem to Solution:

- Grabber statement.
- Problem – Be sure to prove that a problem exists. This could be a big part of the presentation. No solution is necessary if the audience doesn't recognize the problem.
- Solution – Use logical and emotional appeals.
- Review – Draw conclusions.
- Memorable statement – Ask for what you want.

Reflective:

- Grabber statement – Get attention.
- Problem – State the problem.
  Develop the problem, proving that it is urgent and a solution must be formed. Agree upon a criteria for evaluating the solutions and making a decision.
- Solution – List the solutions, starting with the weakest. Evaluate each solution against the criteria which was agreed upon. Discuss the positive aspects first,

then hit the negatives. The negatives must outweigh the positives. After each solution has been smashed, put it to rest. End with the solution you want. Start with any negatives, then end with the positive elements of your solution and why it best meets the criteria.

- Close – Review one more time why your solution will solve the problem.
- Call to action – Ask for what you want.

Motivated Sequence:
- Grabber statement.
- Need – Create pain. If the audience doesn't "feel" the need, you won't be able to satisfy it.
- Satisfaction – Talk about how your plan satisfies the need. Use logic and emotion.
- Visualization – Paint a positive picture of the benefits of your plan.
- Call to action – Get a commitment for something.

Part Five

The Three Main Parts Of Your Presentation

"Every time I play, in my own mind I'm the favorite."
– **Tiger Woods,** 1997 Masters Champion

Most presentations can be organized into three main parts: the introduction, the body and the conclusion.

The introduction

Your introduction should tell the audience members what you are going to be talking to them about. If you will be speaking for 30 minutes, your introduction should last for approximately three or four minutes, about 10 percent of your presentation.

The introduction is your chance to make a dynamic first impression, and as the saying goes, "There are no second chances to make a first impression." Your introduction will serve four purposes:

1. Get the audience's attention

2. Establish WIIFT (What's In It For Them)
3. Establish your credibility and create rapport
4. Let the audience members know what your subject is
   and when they can ask questions

Get the audience's attention

You must grab your audience's attention right away. If you start out slowly, you may never get audience members' attention. The best way to focus attention on you is by using a grabber statement or hook to reel them in. This can take many forms. You can tell a story, give an example, ask a hypothetical question, make a controversial statement, use a quote or use humor. Here are some examples of grabbers that will surely get an audience's attention.

Ask a question. If your speech is about a new substitute for butter, you might begin with this question: "How many of you miss eating butter because you are afraid of having too much fat in your diet?" or, "Would you be willing to try a new food that tastes exactly like butter, but has no fat in it at all?" By asking a question, you give your audience something to quickly think about. In this case, audience members are thinking, "What could really taste like butter but not contain any fat?"

State an unusual fact. Sticking with the butter substitute, you might start with a statistic like this: "There are 65 butter substitutes on the market and not one of them really tastes like butter or has no fat at all."

Give an illustration, example or story. Paint a mental picture for your audience members by telling them a story that relates to your subject. This will get their attention and make the content real for them. For example: "Our company has spent the past 25 years trying to create a substitute for butter which actually tastes like the real thing, but has no fat at all. We have finally succeeded."

Use a quotation. Catchy phrases and quotes can be great openers as long as it's not a quote that has been overused. Go to the library or search the Internet for unusual quotes, or quotes from unusual people.

Use humor. If you are going to try humor, be sure it is in good taste and relevant to your speech. Also be sure that you are comfortable using humor, and it's funny. When in doubt, try it out on someone you trust. Using humor in front of a large audience is very tricky; you don't know who you might offend. Humor does not translate well between cultures or even between regions. What's funny in your town might be offensive to the people where you are speaking.

WIIFT (What's In It For Them)

Don't wait very long to get to this point or you will lose your audience's attention very quickly. If audience members have been told to attend your presentation, or if they are there reluctantly, they will be fidgeting in their seats until they find out whether or not there is some benefit for them in your presentation. If you haven't convinced them in the first few minutes of your presentation that they will derive some benefit, you will have an almost impossible task ahead of you. Pique their interest quickly. If you notice someone leaving the room, don't let it throw you. People leave presentations for many different reasons. Concentrate on making it the best presentation possible for those who are there to listen to you.

Let them know who you are

If everyone in the room already knows who you are, you can skip this step. If not, you need to establish your credentials early on. Let them know why they should be listening to you. Talk about yourself in relation to the topic you will be speaking about. When someone introduces you and lists your credentials, don't repeat them. Give the audience some reasons to want to listen to you. Although I have been introduced many times, I always try to add something at the beginning of my speech that wasn't part of the introduction. Sometimes I refer to something that might have just happened to me, or an experience that sets the tone for my presentation. For example: "A casual conversation with a stranger led me to leave teaching and start my own company." That statement is a grabber on its own, but it also begins an anecdote that I use to explain how I began my company. If you are speaking at a big conference or meeting and you will be introduced, prepare your own introduction and send or fax it to the person who will be introducing you. Bring an extra copy to the event. Ask them to read what you wrote – that way you get the setup you want. If the group already knows you, there is no need to introduce yourself.

Preview your subject

Although your audience members probably know the title or theme of your presentation, and may have a general idea of what it is about, it will help them to hear from you what you are going to be talking about. If you are giving an informative presentation, tell the audience what you want to accomplish. Be direct and keep it short. If your goal is to persuade, you do not have to be quite so specific. You can list several of the points you will be covering, and build up to where you want them to go during your presentation. It's always a good idea for you to tell the audience when you will take questions. The perfect time to do this is in the preview.

What you want to avoid in the introduction is: "Good morning, my name is _____ and I am so glad to be here talking to you today about _____." Audience members either know your name or don't care. Besides, when speakers start, the first few seconds are lost because the audience isn't quite listening yet. "I am glad to be here" – they don't care! They are here for themselves, not for you. "I will be talking about ... ." Audience members also know that. Use the opening to break their preoccupation, get them excited because your presentation hits their needs, and create rapport – all before giving them the content. The opening is the most important part of a presentation.

The Body

The body of the presentation (about 80 percent) is when you tell audience members what you are going to say to them. You should use three to five main points, support them with data and use transitions to connect your material. You may write out your transitions, but use phrases for the main points. The method of organization you choose for the body of your presentation will be determined by the type of presentation, and which best meets your objectives. In the body you will answer the audience members' question "WIIFM?" (What's In It For Me?). The body of your presentation will contain elements to satisfy both the emotional and logical needs of the audience. It may contain new material and/or material that may be familiar but is presented in a new way. Be selective. Not all of the information you have is important enough to be included. It is worthwhile to keep idea files. Whenever you find a newspaper, magazine or journal article, or hear something you would like to remember, put it into this idea file. Don't trust your memory. I was once told a story that was so incredible I wanted to use it in a seminar I was leading later that week. I didn't write it down because I was sure I would remember it. The day of the seminar, I went blank on the story and couldn't tell it to the class. That night I called the person who told me the story, asked her to please repeat it, and wrote it down. It's a story I still tell in my seminars, but it's written down in my files, just in case.

You can add interest to your presentation by using one

or more of the following:

- Examples – add interest
- Stories – let the audience share others' experiences
- Quotations – must be a well-known and reputable source to have value
- Definitions – can help you prove a point or make a point easier to understand
- Comparisons – present similarities
- Contrasts – present differences
- Statistics – numerical facts and figures supporting your points
- Analogies
- Metaphors
- Humor
- Audience involvement
- Visual aids

Using transitions

To achieve continuity as you move from one part of your presentation to another, use transitional phrases. These are short remarks that will move you from the introduction to the body of your presentation and from the body to the conclusion. You may also use them to move from point to point within the presentation. Transitional phrases should be written out in your speech notes. Helpful transitional phrases are "Now that we have looked at ... let's move on to ..." or "We have established the criteria for ... we can now look at ..."

Using supporting materials in the body:

Although you may not be able to convince a hostile audience that your town would benefit by building a skateboard park, using supporting materials can help you go a long way toward making your point. Begin to collect information as soon as you have selected your topic. Write down everything you know on the subject, what the main points are, and what you need to find out. Be sure that your data is current and accurate. Get as much information as possible to support your position.

Validate your point of view

Although it may be a hard sell to convince the taxpayers of your town that a skateboard park is worthwhile, facts and statistics that back up your point of view can help to persuade a skeptical audience of the validity of your arguments. Use facts that parallel your situation. If a nearby community with a similar tax structure has built a skateboard park and if the community as a whole has had significant benefits, outline them in your speech. Have accidents caused by and to skateboarders decreased because they are off the town streets and in a safe location? Have homeowners benefited from safer streets? These are the kinds of supporting facts that can help you to strengthen your presentation.

Add interest

Using tax money to provide recreational facilities that primarily benefit only certain children is not an easy sell. Using data will add interest: the number of families who have children that skateboard, the number of accidents caused by unsafe skateboarding, the nuisance to local shopkeepers and homeowners, the fear of hitting a skateboarder when driving in your town, the low cost of building a skateboard park compared with the cost of auto and medical bills caused by skateboarding accidents.

Audience involvement

Make the audience part of your presentation by using the data to involve them. For example, when speaking about building a skateboard park, you could ask audience members, "How many of you have children who skateboard or have friends who skateboard?" or "How many of you would feel safer driving around town with skateboarders off the streets?" After seeing their response, you could then quote the statistics of what happened in towns where skateboard parks have already been constructed. Other ways to involve members of an audience include: using their names, asking rhetorical and real questions, using their examples, having them do something.

Look for an emotional connection

If you were to give a presentation on home fire safety, your points would be remembered if you mentioned published stories of losses that occurred in your area when smoke detectors were not installed or not working in the home. Examples of stories and people who make events memorable can help you to make your own presentation memorable.

Must know, should know, could know

Since most presentations run longer than speakers anticipate, be prepared to cut some material if needed. An easy way to accomplish this is to color-code your presentation into three sections: Must Know, Should Know, Could Know. Choose a different color marker for each section, so you know immediately which section to eliminate if needed. On your outline, put a box around the "Could Know" section, so you can eliminate it first if necessary. Make sure you remember which color is for which section. If you think you might forget, make yourself a color key at the top of your notes. Then you will only have to glance at the correctly colored section to cut your talk. Don't speak faster to try and get all the information in. It will make your audience members nervous, and in your hurry you may confuse them or leave out important information. With the color-coded method, you will be prepared in the event you have to shorten your presentation.

The conclusion

The last 10 percent of your presentation is the conclusion. It is when you tell the audience members what you have told them. This is the last thing the audience will hear, so you want it to be memorable. It should neatly tie together everything that came before. Be sure to review your main points, and include a strong call to action if you want audience members to do something as a result of your speech. Inexperienced or nervous presenters often miss their final and possibly best opportunity to make their point with the audience. An effective conclusion should emphasize the key points made earlier in your presentation. If you have been giving a sales presentation, this is the time to repeat the product benefits and the benefits to the customer when he or she buys. If you have been motivating taxpayers to fund a skateboard park, this is your last chance to call them to action and have them sign your petition. Your conclusion should also provide closure to your presentation and end by giving the audience something to remember. The famous conclusion to John F. Kennedy's inaugural address in 1961 is one of the most quoted historical statements: "Ask not what your country can do for you, ask what you can do for your country." Short, to the point, and memorable. Your closing may not be as memorable as JFK's, but it should have an impact on your audience.

When creating your own memorable close, follow the examples used in the opening: ask a question; state an unusual fact; give an illustration, example or story; or present a quotation. If you use your opening grabber, add a new ending or insight. For example: "If you want your streets and your children to be safer, support the statistics presented here tonight, and vote 'yes' on the new skateboard park."

Guidelines for effective conclusions

- Your conclusion needs to wrap things up for the audience

- The conclusion should suggest action or next steps
- The conclusion should be 10 percent or less of your presentation
- Your style should be consistent with the rest of your presentation
- Write out the first and last sentences of your conclusion and outline the rest
- End your conclusion on a positive note
- Test your conclusion by asking yourself these questions:
  1. Does my conclusion help listeners get to where I want them to be?
  2. Does it help finish my presentation instead of leaving audience members unsure of what I intended them to know or do?

If the answers to these questions are "yes," then your conclusion meets the criteria for success.

Ten steps to an organized speech

1. Select the topic. Make sure it is appropriate for the audience. (Remember your PAL™).

2. Limit the topic to one central theme, keeping in mind the amount of time you have to make your presentation and the level of the audience you will be addressing.

3. Gather the information. Write down everything you know about the topic, then evaluate what you need to research. Remember to include more than just facts and figures – use examples, stories, analogies, case studies, quotes, humor and the best type of visual aids for your presentation.

4. Outline your main points. Use between three and five main points in the body of your speech to support your central theme. Add transition sentences to connect the ideas.

5. Collect supporting data. Enhance key points with interesting secondary information to help your audience retain information.

6. Design the introduction. Make sure it's catchy and tells audience members WIIFT (What's In It For Them). Include a grabber or hook to get their attention.

7. Write a strong conclusion. Lead the audience by referring to your introduction, reviewing key points or delivering a call to action.

8. Put together a final draft. Outline your speech on note paper using large print (avoid index cards; they are hard to use in a presentation). Use only the top two-thirds of each page and leave room in the margins for notes. Use either single words or short phrases. Write out your memorable phrases and transitions.

9. Practice your presentation three to six times out loud. Say it differently each time to keep the spontaneity. Tape-record your practice and make any necessary changes.

10. Practice again in front of an audience similar to the real audience. Practice the questions and answers. Remember: Practice does not make perfect, it makes permanent. Perfect practice makes perfect.

Sample speech outline (speech to convince)

Audience: Residents of Newark, New Jersey. Favorable

mix (favorable, uninformed, apathetic).

Purpose: After hearing my speech, the audience will understand why the police Vest-A-Cop program is so important, and believe it is necessary.

Logistics: 30-minute speech, early morning meeting, overhead projector.

I. Introduction

    A. In cities with Vest-A-Cop programs, police officer fatalities and injuries have been significantly reduced.

    B. Newark has had a Vest-A-Cop program for three years, and police are very enthusiastic about it.

    C. In prior years, many officers were injured. In the five years before the Vest-A-Cop program, six officers were fatally wounded.

    D. This program is working very well in Newark.

II. Body

    A. Your tax dollars pay for some of the vests.
        1. Tax revenue accounts for 50 percent of the funds.
        2. Newark residents' personal donations fund 25 percent of the program.
        3. Fund-raisers pay the balance.

    B. An added benefit to the residents of Newark as a result of the program has been a reduced crime rate in the city.
        1. Violent crime has gone down.

2. Police officers are able to patrol on foot more frequently since they got the vests.

Transition: Now that we have seen how beneficial the Vest-A-Cop program is for both officers and citizens, we should consider expanding the program.

C. Newark should be proud of its success; can we improve on our current statistics?
1. Our police force is safer; now we are safer.
2. Expanding the program to our suburbs is something to evaluate.

Transition: The Vest-A-Cop program currently costs each taxpayer $1.50 per year. A police officer out on disability leave costs each of us $25 per year. Vest-A-Cop benefits everyone: We are doing something beneficial for our officers, our community and ourselves.

D. It is far less expensive for us to fund additional Vest-A-Cop programs than to pay out disability for each injured officer, or risk officers' lives.
1. An additional program would cost taxpayers another 50 cents per year.
2. More well-protected police may further reduce our crime statistics.
3. No downside.

III. Conclusion (review and memorable statement)

A. Like its counterparts in other parts of the country, Newark's Vest-A-Cop program is a huge success.

B. We should all think about expanding the program to further protect our police officers and ourselves.

Writing your final draft

You have now spent a considerable amount of time organizing your presentation. The purpose is clear, you have completed an audience analysis and you know what the logistics of the speaking situation will be. It's time to construct the final draft of your speech.

I strongly advise you to make a copy of your final draft. Things get lost, thrown away, even stolen. Leave a copy of your speech with someone who will be available to fax or send it to you, just in case.

I recommend the following format for your final draft:

1. Use 8 1/2 x 11 inch paper; not index cards as they tend to get mixed up and are hard to read.
2. Write on only the top two-thirds of the page so your eye doesn't move down or you drop your chin, which makes your voice go down.
3. To make the final draft readable, use at least 18- to 24-point-size, bold letters. Or, if you are handwriting, use a medium point, felt-tip pen rather than a ballpoint pen.
4. Decide where to use visual aids; make notes in the margins of your draft.
5. Color-code your presentation: could know, should know, must know.

Your outline may consist of words in chronological order where each word leads to a body of thought, or it may be in the form of sentences that provide more information. The drawback with single words is you may forget what you want to say. The drawback with sentences is you may start reading them exactly as written. A better choice is to use short phrases that have enough information to keep your speech on track and not enough to cause you to read them verbatim. You can write out your opening grabber, your transitions and any facts or figures you must include, along with the final close.

Once you have written your final draft, practice your speech at least three times to check for the following:

- Is it clear?
- Is it concise?
- Is it complete?
- Is it correct?

Steps to practice

I have heard thousands of presentations from students in the college classroom as well as in my corporate programs. Given equally well-prepared materials, what separates the good presenters from the rest is the amount of time spent practicing their presentations. Even the most interesting speech will fall flat if it isn't delivered well. And the primary reason that happens is not practicing properly – or practicing enough. Here are my recommendations for practice:

- Practicing in your head isn't practicing. We are all quite eloquent in our minds. However, when we speak out loud something entirely different comes out. The only way to practice correctly is to practice out loud.

- Practice your presentation differently each time, you say it. If you practice it the same way each time you destroy any freshness or spontaneity in your delivery.

- If your presentation is complicated or technical, practice saying it to a spouse or friend who is most like your intended audience to gauge how easily the material is to understand.

- After practicing several times, try practicing just the rough spots. Try those along with your opening and closing statements, key points and transitions until you are comfortable with them.

- Practice in the same way you will be presenting. If you will be standing, then stand. If you will be seated, sit.

- Tape-record yourself after you have practiced out loud several times. As you listen, ask yourself if you would enjoy this presentation if you were a member of your audience. If you wouldn't, it's time to re-write and practice again. Work on your timing.

- Practice with your visual aids. During your last few practice sessions, use whatever aids or handouts you will be using during your presentation. This serves as a final check of whether you have too many visuals or not enough. There is still time for you to change things and make final adjustments. You also need to be familiar with the equipment.

- Do a dress rehearsal. Set up an area with a similar seating arrangement. Wear the clothes you plan to wear to the presentation. If possible, have a live audience or at least one person who is similar to your real audience. Give your entire presentation, including taking questions from the "audience." Ask for feedback and make any last-minute corrections.

- Use every opportunity to practice. A perfect time is when you are driving in the car. You can speak out loud and play audio tapes you have made of your practice sessions.

Practice on-site

If possible, it is advisable to practice your presentation in the room where you will be giving it. This will enable you to check your equipment and get comfortable in the room. If using a podium or lectern, make sure it is placed where you want it. If someone will be speaking before you, note where you want the lectern placed in case it is moved prior to your presentation. Standing behind the lectern for any length of time is frowned upon. It separates you from your audience when your objective is to bring yourself closer to it. Step out from behind the podium and move closer to the audience. If you need to refer to your notes, walk behind it again for a short time. Speakers who spend their entire presentation behind the podium are perceived as aloof. Speakers of short stature sometimes cling to the lectern because of the riser placed behind it to make them tall enough to be seen. A better choice would be to walk forward and stand closer to the audience. It will help to establish a good rapport with them. If you are forced to stand behind the lectern because that is where the microphone is located, consider requesting the use of a wireless microphone or buy your own. If you haven't used a wireless microphone before, familiarize yourself with it well in advance of your presentation so you are not fumbling and can turn it off and on with ease. Remember to turn it off as you leave the platform so that any private remarks you may make are not overheard by the audience. There are several different kinds of microphones on the market today. Get comfortable with as many models as you can, as you may not know what is available where you are presenting. Or, bring your own along.

On the day of your presentation:

1. Arrive early and check the room, locate electrical outlets and test them. Distribute any handouts.
2. Test your equipment; check bulbs. Know how to contact the audiovisual people.
3. If necessary, have telephone calls rerouted or unplug any phones in the room.
4. Locate restrooms.
5. Check seating and rearrange if necessary.
6. Make sure your visual aids can be seen from every seat. Check the lighting.
7. Make sure you can be heard from the back of the room.
8. Set up your visual aids, tape wires down if needed.

9. Do body warm-ups, stretches, relaxation exercises (which will be explained in more detail in chapter 6).
10. Check your appearance; make any necessary adjustments.
11. Greet your audience.

Delivery techniques

Different speaking situations call for different delivery techniques. These techniques are identified as Impromptu, Extemporaneous, Expromptu, Manuscript and Memorized.

Impromptu style

Also known as "off the cuff," impromptu speeches are given on the spur of the moment – occasions such as meetings when you were not previously informed that you would be speaking or when you are asked to give a status report, comment on a proposal, or just share your opinion about the topic under discussion. Many presentations are impromptu, and you can be prepared to present even when you haven't had any advance notice. The secret to being successful at impromptu speaking is to relax and let your knowledge of the subject work for you. If you are going to a meeting, come prepared, just in case you may be called upon for your input and opinions. That way it won't come as a surprise when you are asked. When you know your subject well, it is easier to relax and speak. If you even suspect that you may be asked for an opinion, do some homework on the topic being discussed so you will be able to add something of value. A good example of this instance would be if you are going to a meeting where the topic is downsizing in your department and you are fairly certain your opinion will be solicited since you are a mid-level manager. Now is the time to jot down your thoughts and be prepared. If you are asked to speak, you are ready. If someone else speaks first and says the same things you were thinking, you will be able to, at the very least, agree or disagree and give your reasons why. Many people use impromptu speaking as a way to test their knowledge and the knowledge of colleagues. Successful impromptu speaking offers you an opportunity to shine, and impress colleagues and perhaps your boss. In group situations, impromptu speaking can become brainstorming sessions resulting in new ideas. If you have very strong opinions on a topic, this is a chance for you to be heard.

Extemporaneous style

This is the delivery style most recommended for speakers. Extemporaneous-style presentations are planned, prepared and practiced. They are polished presentations which may be given many times, but should never be exactly the same. You may use an outline or notes, but the speech should never be written out or memorized. An extemporaneous speech may sound spontaneous, but it isn't. Each and every detail has been planned in advance – including anecdotes and illustrations used to make your points. Because what you want to say is planned, you are able to change things around to adapt to your particular audience each time the presentation is given. Politicians frequently give extemporaneous speeches. For example, politicians frequently speak on the same subjects, but they tailor their style and anecdotes specifically for the region they are visiting. If they are in an urban area, they use urban examples; in a farm area, rural ones.

Expromptu style

A combination of extemporaneous and impromptu styles of delivery, the expromptu speech is prepared but not practiced. Unfortunately, this happens too often in corporate America. People wait too long to prepare and then run out of time to practice. Other occasions when you could be asked to give an expromptu presentation may be at a meeting, conference or debate. When you are asked to participate, take some time to put your thoughts together, even though you have no time to practice. Your success as an expromptu speaker depends on how well you gather and organize your thoughts. On these occasions, you still have time to write an opening sentence that will set you up to make your points. Use notes to help organize your thoughts. Write a closing sentence to end your presentation; this will also serve to let your audience know you have finished speaking.

Manuscript style

A manuscript speech is written down and read word for word to the audience. It is widely used in the scientific community where technical papers, requiring exact wording, are submitted for presentation, accepted and then read by the author. Politicians and many CEOs use manuscript speeches when they want their exact words to be used. It is also the style employed by people who use TelePrompTers™. This format also ensures exact adherence to a timetable that can be essential when each speaker has a limited amount of time available for his or her presentation. Because listening to a speech being read can be dull for the audience, it is essential to have copies of your speech for handouts. You can use visual aids with a manuscript speech to help make it more interesting for the audience. Unless you have to use the manuscript style, it is best to avoid it. If you have material that has to be presented exactly as written, do so, but try to paraphrase the rest of the speech. If you must read from a manuscript, use the scope technique – slide your thumb and pointer finger down the page, scoping one section at a time. This will help you to find your place after you look up at the audience. It is critical that the manuscript is easy to read. Use a combination of upper and lower case letters, fonts that are 24-point-size, and mark the script with underlines for key words to emphasize, spaces for pause, etc. Manuscript presentations require a great deal of practice.

Memorized style

Unless you are a professional actor who can memorize speeches and make them sound like you just came up with the thoughts, forget about memorized-style presentations. Most people cannot memorize every word they have written. And, there are obvious differences between orally spoken language and written words. Typically, people do not speak the way they write. Oral language consists of short sentences and phrases, contractions, slang, and starts and stops. Written language consists of longer, more formal sentences with transitions. What's written on paper may look OK, but it doesn't sound so good when you speak the same words. The most painful public speaker to watch is one who has written a speech, thinks he or she has it memorized, gets up to the podium and forgets it. Because of the way the presentation has been prepared, he or she is unable to go on or even come up with an alternate opening line. There is little chance of success with a memorized speech. As a speaker, you depend on cues from people in the audience to guide your delivery, adapting it when necessary to meet their needs. You will not be able to do this with a memorized presentation, and you will be leaving yourself open to failure.

The five styles of delivery & when to use them

Style	Description	When To Use It
Impromptu	Off the cuff	Spur of the moment
Extemporaneous	Planned, prepared practiced	Planned events
Expromptu	Prepared, not practiced	Meetings, short notice
Manuscript	Written, read word for word	Scientific and political conferences (when exact wording is critical)
Memorized	Recited word for word	Never!

Part Six

Stage Fright & How To Control It

"Fear is a huge factor in diving. It's a part of the sport, it's a part of overcoming the sport, it's a part of the thrill of the sport."
– **Michele Mitchell-Rocha,** Olympic silver medal winner

You have a problem. You are one of the millions of people who are frightened to speak in public. You are not alone. Whether this is your first presentation, or number 100, almost everyone suffers from some level of stage fright or performance anxiety. Actors suffer from the same feelings, and many say they never get over them. What they have learned, and what you can learn, is to take those feelings and use them to your advantage. Although, in surveys, the fear of speaking in public ranks ahead of death, flying, heights and snakes, this fear can be controlled. It is a perfectly normal feeling, and a form of energy that can be channeled to your benefit. To use these feelings to your own advantage, first you must identify them. There are four common fears that most speakers have:

1. Fear of fainting. Unless you have a medical problem, this is almost unheard-of. You may feel faint, but it is highly unlikely that you will faint.

2. Fear of boring your audience. If you approach speaking as an audience-centered sport, you will seldom need to be concerned with boring your audience. Make sure that:

- Your material is interesting and you have backed it up with facts, figures and anecdotes to enhance and illustrate your points.
- You are speaking directly to each person in the audience.
- You are enthusiastic about the topic, and your voice and body language shows it.

3. Fear of your mind going blank. This can happen. We have all seen it happen to other people, and you need to learn what to do if it happens to you: Pause, look at your notes or outline and try to pick up again where you left off, or move on to your next thought. Don't be afraid to use your notes to get back on track. If you realize a mistake was made during your presentation, correct it if it will have impact on the audience, or let it slide if it is something unimportant.

4. Fear of being judged. If you are well-prepared and have practiced enough, everything should go smoothly. It is important that the audience knows you enjoy your subject, even if you've made some mistakes or have lost your place. A sincere presenter doing his or her best, who is obviously well-prepared, will not be judged harshly.

Once you have identified your fears, begin working to manage them and let them help you. First, accept that stage fright is a normal feeling, experienced by most people. Next, observe how other speakers handle their anxiety or ask them what they do to relax before a presentation. Perhaps you've noticed speakers doing breathing exercises, or shoulder and head rolls before their presentations. Many speakers have brief exercise routines that help them relax. Others use self-talk to turn the fear into excitement. An important aspect of fear control is to speak frequently. The more you practice, the better speaker you will become.

Self-talk builds self-esteem

The conversations you have with yourself build or destroy your self-image. If you can regulate your self-talk to upgrade your self-image, you can convince yourself of almost anything. If you walk into a presentation believing you are going to fail, you probably will. But if you do as I do, and give yourself a positive self-talk, your chances for success will increase drastically. I frequently use the self-talk mantra created by speech expert Dorothy Sarnoff. It goes like this: "I'm glad I'm here. I'm glad you're here. I care about you. I know that I know." I repeat this mantra over and over to myself until I am relaxed. The message you are sending to yourself is one of joy and ease. It expresses your pleasure in being there to present. It says, "I'm thinking about you." And it communicates that you have taken the time and effort to prepare a presentation worth giving and worth listening to. Every time you arrive at a presentation repeat this mantra to yourself. Say it silently or out loud, fast or slow, it doesn't matter. It will become a chant allowing you to entertain only positive thoughts and messages. Positive self-talk is an effective means of controlling stage fright.

Visualization

Another effective way to control stage fright is by using visualization. In the visualization process, you picture yourself in front of an audience. You are composed, confident and in control. You see yourself delivering a presentation, and in your mind's eye, you watch yourself as you successfully reach out to the audience and deliver an audience-centered presentation. You need not go further than your introduction, but you may want to include a positive response by the audience. By picturing yourself in a successful situation, you are able to give yourself the confidence you need to achieve your goal.

Staying in control

Positive self-talk and visualization are tools to help you control your stage fright, but there are some basic rules to follow which will make controlling your fears easier. Arrive early. Get to where you are presenting with lots of time to spare. This will give you a chance to relax, survey your surroundings, make a trip to the restroom, organize your thoughts and check the facilities as well as any equipment you may be using. The speaker who rushes in at the last minute does himself or herself a disservice. We all need the time to mentally prepare ourselves for the event at hand.

Eat lightly. Before you are going to present, it is best to avoid heavy meals. This also means no alcohol, and nothing that might cause your stomach to be upset. Bananas are a good choice, they are light and filling. It is also important to avoid taking decongestants or other medications that might make you drowsy. You don't want to appear tired during your presentation.

Use humor to help release endorphins. Listen to a funny tape on the way to your presentation and let yourself laugh. Laughter is a great tension reliever.

Take some of the pressure off yourself by using interactive techniques. When you begin your presentation, plan to ask audience members a question and get them to raise their hands. Or have them make a sound, or any other interactive device you can think of. This will take some of the focus off you and put it onto them. You can use these moments to take a deep breath and relax.
Another way to help you relax before your presentation is to try the simple exercise routine that I use before I speak. It can be done just about anywhere; I've even done it on an airplane!

Brody's basics

The "rag doll": Stand up straight with your feet comfortably apart. Stretch up tall, then bend over by collapsing quickly and loosely from the waist with your arms relaxed and hands dangling. Keep your arms, hands and neck relaxed so you look like a rag doll. Do not bounce. Wait 10 seconds. Now, slowly rise up to a straight position, keeping relaxed. Repeat five times.

Head rolls: Immediately after the rag doll, while your neck is still relaxed, stand straight with your hands close to your chest. Begin to slowly rotate your neck first to the left, then forward with your chin down in front, then to the right. Don't roll your neck back. Then do this again; reverse the rotation rolling to the right, then front, then left, then front. Be sure your neck is relaxed. Repeat five times.

Arm swings: After the head roll, stand straight with your arms to your sides. Swing your left arm in a large circle from front to back, as if you were doing the back stroke. Swing your right arm in a large circle from front to back in the same manner. Reverse and swing your left arm in a large circle from back to front. Do the same with your right arm. Swing your arms in this manner five times on each side.

Shoulder shrugs: Right after the arm swings, stand straight with your arms at your sides. Using your arms, move your shoulders straight up to the level of your ears. Drop your shoulders back down to their resting position. Shrug your shoulders four more times.

Yawning: After completing the rag doll and the head

rolls, your face and neck muscles and vocal chords should be relaxed. Now, standing straight, slowly yawn, sounding an "ahhhhh" on exhalation. The sound you make is a relaxed sound. Strive for this relaxed and open quality whenever you speak.

Abdominal breathing: Sit upright in a chair and place both feet flat on the floor. Rest your hands in your lap. Take a deep breath through the nose while extending your stomach. Push your stomach out as the air comes into and fills your lungs. Your shoulders can rise and may possibly go back a bit. Place one hand on your chest and the other on your abdomen. Which hand rises most? If it is the hand on your abdomen, you are breathing properly. If not, pull your breath deeper into your lungs. Once your lungs are full, hold the air to the count of six and then let the air escape from your nose. Repeat, taking each deep breath slowly through the nose. Do this 10 times.

Brody's basic refreshers

If you find you need a quick refresher before giving your presentation, here are two that you can do even while seated at your table or on the dais.

Deep breathing I: Take a deep breath in through your nose and tighten everything in your body, from your head, neck, shoulder, hands, fingers, legs and toes. Hold the breath for six seconds, then slowly let go of the tension in your body as you exhale through your mouth to a count of 10.

Deep breathing II: Take a deep breath and clasp your hands together. Hold your breath as you squeeze your palms together tightly. Let go of your hands and breath at the same time.

Both of these deep breathing refreshers help you to slow your heartbeat. As you do this, you will also slow down the surge of adrenaline that is making you tense.

How to handle stage fright

1. Accept the fact that stage fright is normal; you may have it every time you speak, but let it work for you by thinking of it as excitement not fear.
2. Watch other speakers and learn their techniques.
3. Concentrate on your strengths, compensate for your weaknesses.
4. Practice, practice, practice before you are going to present. Remember, perfect practice makes perfect presentations.
5. Speak often; the more you speak the better you will be able to manage your stage fright.

Managing the physical symptoms of stage fright

For dry mouth:
- No milk products, soda, alcoholic beverages, caffeine, sugar
- Lightly coat your teeth with petroleum jelly (Vaseline™); it will stop your lip from sticking to your teeth
- Bite the tip of your tongue (this helps you to salivate)

- Drink room temperature or warm water (with lemon, if available)

For sweaty hands/body:
- Use talcum powder or cornstarch on hands/body
- Carry a handkerchief

If you have red splotches on your face:
- Wear pink or red colors
- Wear high necklines
- Use humor to release endorphins

If your voice is shaky: Project your voice to the back row of the audience

If your hands are shaky: Gesture

If your legs are shaky or your knees are knocking: Move

If your heartbeat is rapid: Do some deep breathing

Part Seven

Platform Skills

"The key for me is to forget about the results and concentrate on execution."
– **Oral Hershiser,** Los Angeles Dodgers

The way we deliver our message to other people is made up of three components, the three V's: Visual, Vocal, Verbal. Each carries a percentage of the listeners' perception of the total message. These are overall percentages which can vary based upon the speaker, the subject and the audience. The visual is what we look at: dress, body language, posture and facial expression. The vocal is your voice and how it sounds to others. The verbal is the words you choose. These three components are far from equally weighted. Since visual has the most initial impact, it is important that you, as a presenter, properly prepare yourself to show your audience a positive visual message.

The visual

Dress for success

How you look can color what people hear you saying. If you have done your homework and researched the audience, you can choose clothing that will enhance your presentation and be appropriate for the occasion. If you are speaking at a conference, ask the color of the backdrop. Avoid what I did – wear a royal blue suit only to find a royal blue background. I blended in and all you could see was a talking head.

For men, a suit demonstrates more authority than a sports coat or blazer. However, if you are in a warm-weather climate, and many members of the audience are wearing short-sleeve shirts or dressing more casually, a suit may make you seem standoffish. When unsure of what to wear, ask the person who has scheduled you to speak, or talk to others in the company. For men, dark colors such as navy blue and charcoal gray communicate power and authority. For big men, black may seem too austere. Keeping the suit jacket closed gives the impression of a broad chest and narrow waist. White or light blue shirts are always appropriate, along with silk ties, high-rise socks and polished dark leather shoes. Many companies have business casual days. As an outside visitor to the firm, this does not apply to you unless requested to wear business casual attire.

Women do not have to dress like men to appear professional; but they do have to look professional. Skirts should not be too short or too tight. Check to see that there are no runs in stockings and carry an extra pair for emergency. Shoes should be conservative with low to medium heels. Jewelry should not clang or dangle. Sweaters should not cling and blouses should not be low-cut. Find out which colors look best on you and wear them. If you are unsure, a professional image or color consultant is a worthwhile person to consult. Make sure your clothes fit properly. If you wear glasses, save the tinted lenses for weekends. People want to see your eyes. No granny glasses. The day of your presentation is not

BUSINESS
PROFESSIONAL
What to do

Limited jewelry

Suit

Conservative heels

BUSINESS
PROFESSIONAL
What to do

Well-fitting suit

Long-sleeve shirt

Jacket buttoned

the time for new shoes, unless you have broken them in first. You don't want to find yourself standing in front of a group with a pained expression because your feet hurt. If you are unsure as to how your clothing looks, have someone view you from all sides – including the rear. Use a full-length mirror to check yourself. Clothing that fits poorly will distract from what you have to say. Audience members may remember your split seam instead of the speech.

Basic traditional business wardrobe for men

- Two-piece *suits*. Several two-button, three-button or double-breasted suits in navy, gray, charcoal or pinstripes. Avoid brown. Double-breasted jackets must be buttoned except when sitting down. Suit jackets should not be worn with other trousers.
- *Sports coats* and *trousers* should contrast for a more casual look.
- *Ties* should be silk or wool. Color and patterns should not be loud or flashy. Burgundy, red and navy work as background colors. Small prints and stripes are good choices. Paisleys are good alternatives. Do not wear a matching handkerchief. A knot should fill the space at the shirt top.
- *Shirts* should be long-sleeved, even in warm weather. Solid colors are preferred. Shirts should be well-pressed. Avoid lavender, peach, plaids, dots and broad stripes.
- Polished leather *shoes* in a dark color (black is best).

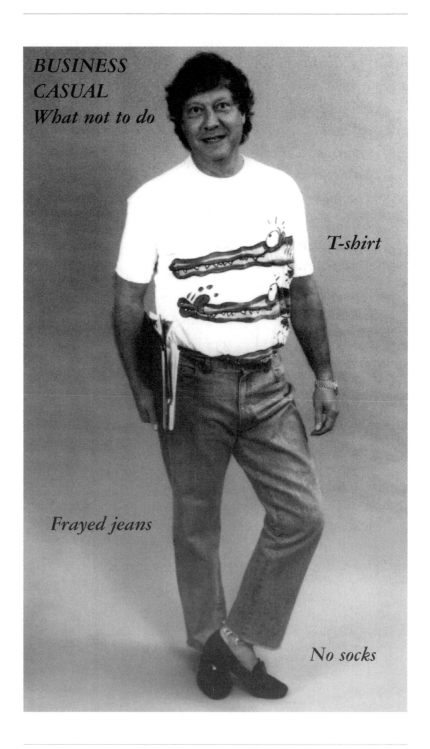

BUSINESS
CASUAL
What not to do

T-shirt

Frayed jeans

No socks

Business casual wardrobe for men

- Chinos or "Dockers"-type trousers
- Sports shirts with collars or banded necks
- Polo shirts with collars
- Sweater or sports jacket
- Casual loafers or lace-up shoes

Basic traditional business wardrobe for women

- Black, navy or gray two-piece suit
- Pantsuit may work depending on your industry
- Contrasting jacket and skirt
- Two-piece dress or dress with jacket
- Several neutral blouses (white/off-white)
- Solid color blouse; may be pastel
- One pair gold, one pair silver earrings
- Scarves that pick up colors from suits or blouses
- Black pumps; navy or taupe pumps
- Neutral or taupe hosiery

Business casual wardrobe for women

- Pantsuit
- Casual skirts or slacks. Neatly pressed chinos or corduroys are acceptable
- Cotton shirts in solids, prints or muted plaids
- Sweaters (not too tight)
- Blazers to wear over slacks or skirts
- Low-heeled shoes or boots
- Stockings or socks

BUSINESS
CASUAL
What not to do

*Exposed
midriff*

*Ripped,
baggy jeans*

*Sandals,
no socks*

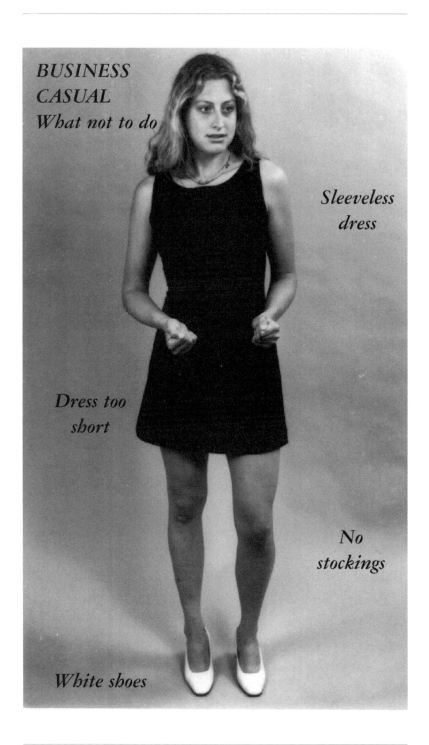

BUSINESS CASUAL
What not to do

Sleeveless dress

Dress too short

No stockings

White shoes

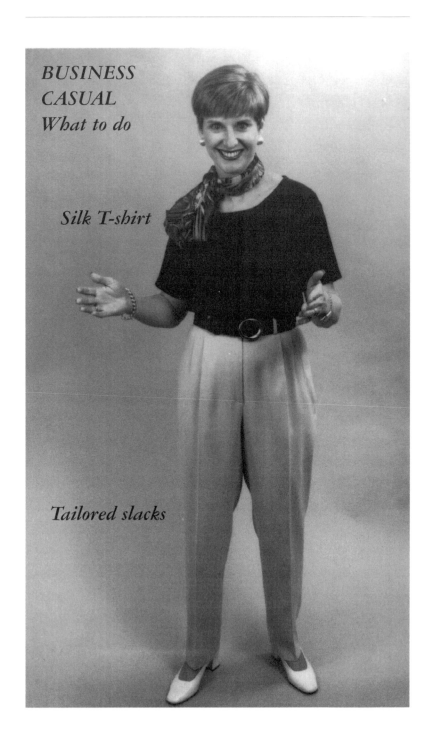

BUSINESS
CASUAL
What to do

Silk T-shirt

Tailored slacks

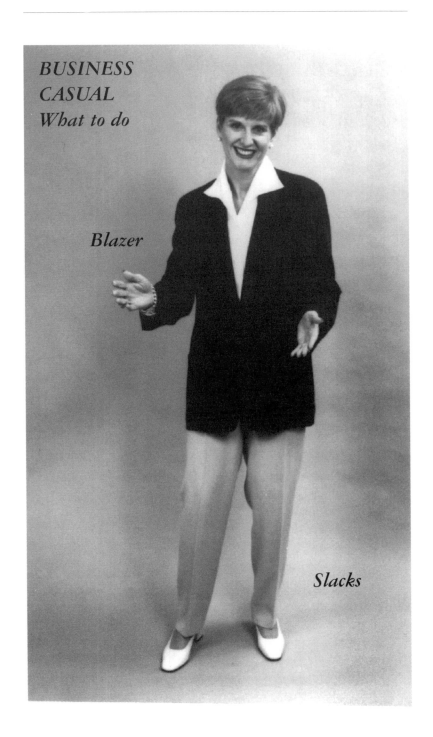

BUSINESS
CASUAL
What to do

Blazer

Slacks

*BUSINESS CASUAL
What to do*

Long- or short-sleeve shirt

Slacks

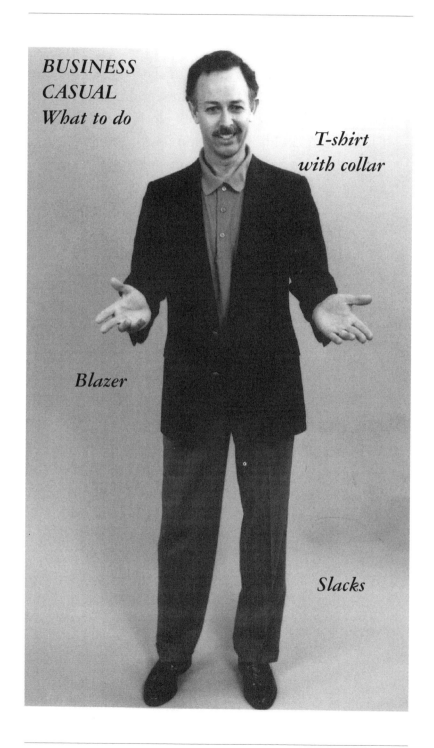

BUSINESS
CASUAL
What to do

T-shirt
with collar

Blazer

Slacks

Grooming guidelines – men & women

- Clean hair; if you spot dandruff flakes, use tape to remove them before your presentation begins
- Clean, well-pressed, unspotted clothing
- Clean, clear eyeglasses (no sunglasses indoors)
- No eyeglasses hanging on chains or other devices
- Polished, clean, white teeth
- Good breath – avoid onion, garlic, dairy products
- Facial hair (and nose hair) trimmed for men, removed for women
- Check a full-length mirror

Posture is important!

Do you slump or slouch? Have you ever been told to stand up straight? To evaluate your own posture, first look at yourself on video or in photographs. If you don't like the way you look, follow these directions:

- Put your feet hip-width apart – keep them parallel facing the audience. Put your weight on the balls of your feet which will throw your knees slightly forward. This will keep you from swaying or shifting your weight.
- Put your arms loosely by your sides.
- Now your shoulders are over your hips, your back is lengthening and widening, and your posture is straight and good.

When you are seated, you want to look energized and confident. You don't want to lean or slouch or appear too comfortable or relaxed. Proper seated posture when

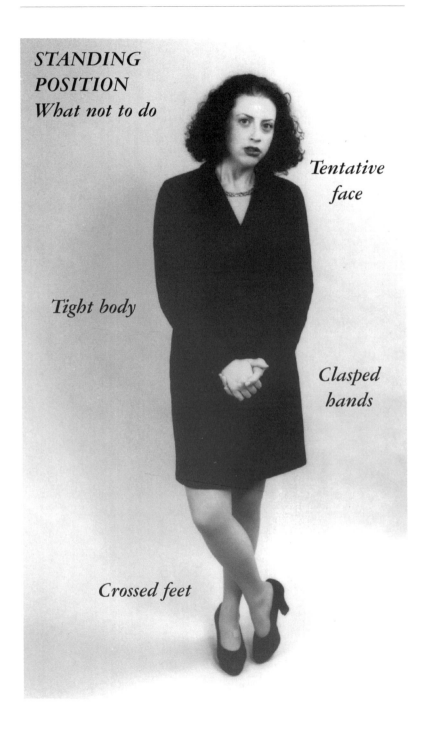

STANDING
POSITION
What not to do

Tentative face

Tight body

Clasped hands

Crossed feet

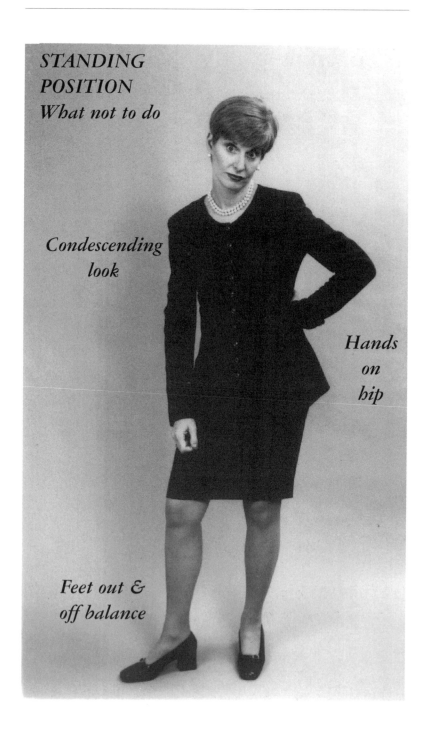

STANDING
POSITION
What not to do

Condescending
look

Hands
on
hip

Feet out &
off balance

STANDING
POSITION
What not to do

Angry face

Crossed arms

Weight off
balance

STANDING
POSITION
What not to do

No eye
contact

Crossed arms

Feet not
balanced

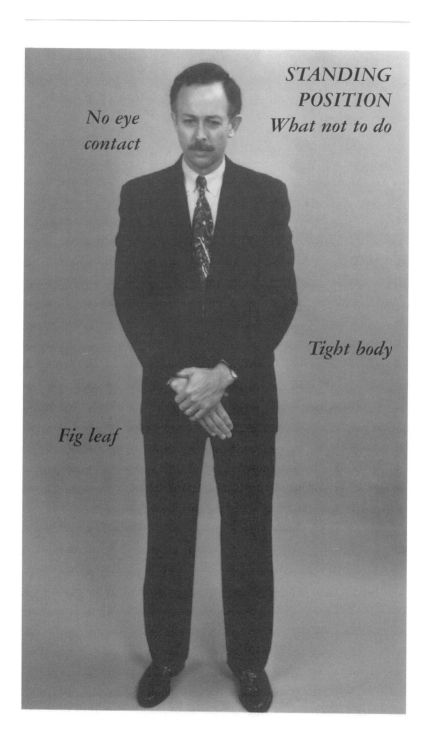

STANDING
POSITION
What not to do

*Scowling
face*

*Parade rest
(no energy)*

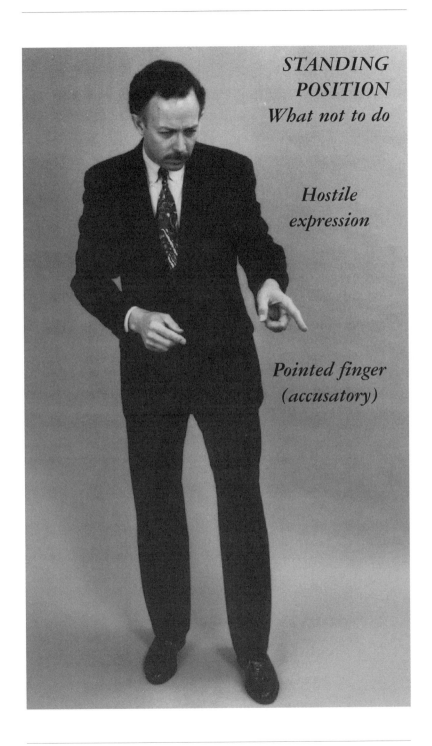

STANDING
POSITION
What not to do

*Hostile
expression*

*Pointed finger
(accusatory)*

STANDING
POSITION
What to do

Open

you are presenting (or just want to look good at a meeting) is sitting straight up in your chair, spine straight, with your feet flat on the floor and hands open on the table.

Posture & movement

Have you ever watched a speaker sway or rock at the podium? It's very distracting and can detract from even the most interesting speech. How you appear to the audience will have an impact on their reaction to what you are going to tell them. Your posture and the way you conduct yourself on the platform is an important part of your presentation. Your objective is to be comfortable and controlled while you are presenting. You want the audience to see that you are relaxed and in control. To achieve a comfortable speaking position, stand up and spread your feet about 6 to 8 inches apart, parallel to each other with toes pointed straight ahead. Flex your knees and put your weight on the balls of your feet. Standing in this position will stop any swaying or rocking motion and will diminish any distracting heel movements.

Comfortable movements will relax both you and your audience. Take at least two steps, and then get back into position. Do not pace, it's distracting. Use movements to establish contact with your audience. You may even want to walk to the side or rear of the room, pause there, speak, and then return to your place in front. Getting physically closer to your audience increases its attention and interest. It also encourages response if you are asking questions. The accepted public distance zone is 12 to 25 feet. In smaller group situations, you can approach within a social distance of 4 to 12 feet primarily, and occasionally get as close as 18 inches to 4 feet. Stand up straight and face the audience head-on. Keep your posture open with arms relaxed and hanging down at your sides. If your arms are crossed in front, it may make you seem defensive. Hold your head up high with your chin up. Having your chin raised gives you the aura of being in control; chin down connotes acquiescence. Visual signals that make you appear not to be in control will detract from your presentation.

The eyes have it

Don't be afraid to make eye contact with audience members. Their reactions to you will help your performance as a presenter. If you sense boredom, you may have to pick up the pace; if you sense enthusiasm, it can help to pump you up. When you make eye contact, you are relating to your audience, which will help get your message across.

In order to make proper eye contact, think of the audience as sitting in a "Z" formation. Start with a familiar or friendly face. Look at that person for three to five seconds, or to complete a thought, and then move to someone else in the room. Don't be predictable. Start in the middle or the back of the room to vary your eye contact. If you make eye contact with someone who quickly turns away, try not to look directly into that person's eyes again. In some cultures, direct eye contact is inappropriate, and some people just feel uncomfort-

SEATED
POSITION
What not to do

Legs on table

Crossed arms

Back in chair

able being looked at. You may also nod occasionally, and you will probably get a nod back, at least if the person agrees with what you just said. If you get a head shake, you'll know who disagrees with you.

Facial expressions

Be aware of your facial expressions. Put a mirror next to your desk at work for one week. Watch your face when you are talking on the telephone. Be aware of any artificial, unfriendly or deadpan expressions you may be making. Do you squint, frown, make strange faces? Once you become aware of the expressions you make, it will be easier for you to eliminate them. Practice smiling and looking pleasant. That's how you want to look during your presentations. It isn't easy to speak and smile at the same time, but it is important to smile during your presentation or at least use facial expressions if they are congruent with your message. Some men find it more difficult to smile while presenting than women do, but practice helps here. Videotape your presentation or practice in front of a friend. Watch your expression and see if you have smiled enough and in appropriate places. If not, you can write reminder notes to yourself in the margin of your speech or just practice smiling beforehand. Women must be careful not to over smile. They may appear to be insipid.

Body language

You're at a meeting and have just been asked for your views. You are unprepared, nervous and want to slump down in your seat so no one will notice you. No matter how nervous you are, now is the time to sit up straight in your chair, keep your hands above the table, use gestures and make eye contact. While you are trying to collect your thoughts, open by paraphrasing the question you have just been asked. This will give you a brief amount of time to think of something to say. Others at the meeting will be responding to your body language. How you look, gesture and make eye contact will be influencing the opinion of others. You don't get a second chance to make a first impression, so the visual message you send must be strong and positive.

Gestures

Gestures are also a part of your visual picture. They are visual reinforcements of the words and ideas you are trying to communicate to your audience. Gestures include hand, arm and head movements and can enhance your presentation or detract from it. Have you ever had a conversation with someone who "talks with their hands?" It some cultures, it is an accepted and commonplace addition to spoken communication. In American culture, some hand gestures such as finger pointing and fist raising can be interpreted as hostile or threatening. When giving presentations, men frequently stand in the "at ease" position commonly used in the military. They cross their hands behind their backs, and keep them there. Or they cross their hands low in front of them like a fig leaf on a statue. Both men and women frequently cross their arms over their chests thinking they appear relaxed and confident. To many in the audience, this stance makes the speaker look merely defensive. By facing audience members with your arms crossed you are closing yourself to them, and they will sense this. Since your objective is to communicate with openness and sincerity, you want to make open gestures to reinforce what you are saying.

Another gesture to avoid is putting your hands in your pockets. Some nervous presenters use this as a way of keeping their shaking hands out of sight, and often wind up jingling their keys or the change in their pockets without realizing it. Some people can't get their hands back out again and wind up spilling the contents of their pockets as they try to release their hands. To avoid embarrassment, it's wise to empty your pockets of change and keys before presenting.

Clasping your hands into a folded position as when praying is another gesture to eliminate. This gesture tightens you up and pulls in your energy instead of releasing it and allowing you to reach out to the audience. A weak twirling motion with your hands or wagging your fingers when making a point also indicates your unease to the audience.

Gestures also help you to emphasize important points during your presentation. They reinforce what you are saying with a visual message. The most effective gestures are spontaneous ones. They come from what you are thinking and feeling, and they help the audience members to relate to you and what you are telling them. It is much more effective to watch a speaker who uses movement than to listen to someone standing behind a lectern with hands clasped in front of him or her.

You can use gestures effectively

Have you ever watched an evangelist on television using wide, sweeping gestures while speaking? These gestures are effective because they include everyone, making viewers feel a part of things even though they are simply watching from their own homes. As a presenter in a business setting, you will be using gestures sparingly to emphasize points in your presentation. But like the TV evangelist, when you gesture, use the upper quadrant of your body, and make your gestures up and out to the audience. Your movements should be broad and flowing, not fast and jerky. The most effective gestures are natural extensions of yourself.

Your gestures should be varied; don't use the same motion over and over again. Repetition can be distracting to audience members and you may find they are watching your gestures instead of listening to the presentation. Some gestures interfere with the audience's ability to pay attention, such as the threatening ones mentioned earlier (finger pointing and fist waving). Instead, use your palms and open them out to your audience. Move your arm and hand as a single unit gesturing up and out toward the audience. Use either one or two arms. Try a sweeping motion and relate the extent of your gestures to the size of your audience. Bigger audiences need bigger gestures. Don't forget that nodding the head and smiling are effective ways to emphasize what you are saying. As a presenter who uses gestures effectively, you will be projecting confidence and competence, and the response you get from your audience will let you know when you have succeeded. Listeners also feel more comfortable with a speaker who uses gestures effectively. Gestures work best when they are natural and spontaneous. Practiced gestures can look stiff and stilted when used during a presentation. You can, however, learn how to gesture effectively.

Practice exercise: Stand in front of a full-length mirror. Get into a comfortable stance. How does it look? Now, separate your feet approximately 6 to 8 inches apart. Drop your arms loosely to your sides. Now practice a variety of gestures. What feels uncomfortable (because it is new) may look terrific. What feels comfortable may look sloppy or tight. Do these exercises three times a week for one minute. Within a month or two, your natural gestures will be more open and fluid.

Keys to effective gesturing

- Use gestures to emphasize major points
- Let your movements be broad and flowing, not fast and jerky
- Vary your gestures
- Don't point your finger or fist – these gestures are intimidating

- Use your palms and open them to your audience
- Move your arm and hand together as a single unit to avoid floppy wrists or elbows
- Use large gestures for a large audience and narrow them for a smaller group
- Evaluate your gestures by doing them in front of a mirror
- Avoid gestures that make you seem nervous or defensive
- Don't stand with your hands behind your back or crossed in front of you
- Don't keep your hands in your pockets
- Keep hands and gestures above your waist
- Gestures should be upward and open

The vocal

Your voice plays a big part of audience perception. When we are stressed, our voices tend to rise, but the deeper the pitch, the longer people will listen to what you have to say. You can learn to gain control over your pitch and bring it into a lower range. Try this exercise: Repeat the following three sentences, each time using a deeper pitch:

"This is my normal pitch."
"Do, Re, Me, Fa, So, La, Ti, Do"
"This is my normal voice."

Stop and listen for differences between the first and last sentences. Repeat the trio of sentences until you are in control of your pitch and can deepen it at will. Practice this exercise 10 times each day, and after six weeks you will have greater control over your pitch.

Volume

Even the most interesting presentation will fail if it can't be heard; conversely, if it is delivered in a very loud voice, the audience will think you are shouting at them. Being able to control your volume, and vary it, will help you hold the audience's attention. To help you control your volume, try this exercise:

Breathe from the diaphragm and speak as if your voice is hitting the back wall of the room you are in. Breathing from the diaphragm allows more airflow and will help to avoid a sore throat when projecting.

Fast talk/slow talk

The normal speaking rate is between 120 and 160 words per minute. If people are always asking you to repeat yourself, you probably talk too fast. If they are usually interrupting you, you probably speak too slowly. To control your rate, read aloud. Take 160 words from any source and time yourself as you read them. Based on the results, you will know whether to slow down or speed up your normal rate. Practice every day until comfortable with your new rate of speech. Rate may need to be varied depending on your audience. Southern audiences use a slower rate than many Northern audiences. When English isn't a first language, the speaker will need to speak more slowly. If the information is very technical, the speaker will need to slow down and pause frequently for the audience to assess the meaning.

Emphasis

When we speak, we tend to emphasize certain words or phrases. In your presentations, the words and phrases you emphasize should be ones that will bring home your point to the audience. You can change the meaning of a sentence simply by changing position of the words you emphasize. The technique used to emphasize words or phrases in your presentation is called "punching it." Many professional speakers and speech writers underline the words and phrases they want to emphasize. You can do the same on your own outline, and when you practice the presentation, practice "punching it" as well. For example, in this sentence the emphasis changes the speaker's intent: "When we deal with companies *your* size ..." compared to "When we deal with companies your *size* ... ."

Pause to punctuate

The pause is as critical in oral language as punctuation is in written language. When you fill pauses with "and," "uh," and "um," it is not only distracting, but also doesn't allow the audience to think about what you are saying. In your mind, when you get to a period, count to three; a colon, count to two; and a comma, count to one. Don't rush your ideas or sound hesitant by using fillers.

Voice problems

Your voice becomes a problem when it calls attention to

itself. There are several common voice problems:

- Harshness – Unless it is physical in nature, a harsh voice indicates tension and stress. Use relaxation techniques to help eliminate the problem. If your throat is dry, drink warm water with lemon before speaking.
- Nasality – frequently caused by speaking with the jaws clenched. It can be reduced by opening the mouth wider and using the tongue more firmly.
- Breathlessness – usually caused by insufficient breathing while speaking. Take deeper breaths and release a controlled flow of air.
- High pitch – unless physical in nature, can be improved with vocal exercises and conscious effort to speak in your lower vocal range.

Finish with strength

Does your voice tend to rise at the end of a sentence? Tape-record yourself speaking the first few lines of your presentation. If your voice goes up at the end of a sentence, it will sound as though you are asking a question or are tentative about what you just said. If you tend to swallow your last few words, that will reduce the impact of what you are saying as well. Finish sentences completely and drop your pitch slightly while keeping the volume strong. Listen to newscasters as they close their broadcasts; most of them use a tag line which they repeat regularly with volume up and pitch down. Practice until comfortable with the way you sound.

The verbal

It may be difficult to accept that after all the hard work and preparation that goes into a presentation, the verbal message or content often accounts for the smallest percent of the impact on most audiences, the vocal and visual claiming the lion's share of the initial, and sometimes long-term, impact. Obviously what you have to say is important, and communicating your ideas clearly and concisely will be the greatest challenge as a presenter. Your audience will be looking for "WIIFM" (What's In It For Me?) from the moment you begin to speak. Make sure your opening tells them what they can expect to get from your presentation. One key to audience acceptance and respect is to talk the way your audience does. It means you should keep the audience in mind when writing your presentation, so you can use familiar words and concepts that will be of interest. Consider using anecdotes to bring yourself into the world of your listeners by relating experiences you may have in common with them. If your presentation is to a technical group, by all means use technical terms and jargon, but using some colorful language as well could make your presentation even more interesting. For all presentations, use simple, descriptive language. Adjust your vocabulary to suit the group. The more you know about who comprises your audience, the easier it will be for you to speak their language. Avoid foreign phrases unless you are planning on translating them for the audience. Keep your sentences and words short. What words can you eliminate to make your speech more concise? If you are using language that can mean different things to different members of the audience, be sure to explain your meaning. For example, "politics" can refer to a system or government, or refer to the inner dynamics of an organization. There is a world of difference between mentioning that a product is "cheap" and saying it is "inexpensive." Be sure you have taken the audience's industry or profession in mind when preparing your presentation. Be sincere and never pretend that you have things in common with your audience when you don't. Be honest. Your words will paint a picture for your listeners, and using colorful and descriptive language will help you bring it to life for them.

Pauses & power robbers

We hear competent speakers every day. Listen to radio or television and you will hear confident, authoritative men and women telling us about the news, current events, or even endorsing products. How do these people sound and what kind of words do they use? The professional speakers in our world use clear, colorful language in short, simple sentences that are easy to understand. All too often our verbal skills distort our images as capable, knowledgeable professionals. We hem and haw, trying to find the right word. We may even discount ourselves and our ideas without realizing it, or we might unknowingly offend others with our language. All of these verbal faults are "power robbers" that detract from our authority, professionalism and power. Hedges and qualifiers are also common power robbers.

These are the filler words we use when we are uncertain about what we have to say. Examples are: "I guess," "I hope," "probably," "kinda," "sorta." "Um," "ah," "like" and "you know" are also distracting and annoying if they are abundant. I recently went to hear a psychologist speak. She had an interesting topic and was a very attractive presenter. Unfortunately, she had a very annoying habit that detracted from her presentation. After the first five minutes, I found myself counting the "ums" in her speech just out of curiosity. I stopped counting at 100.

Passive sentences are also power robbers. Active sentences show we took the initiative and performed an action. Passive sentences and words say that things happened to us or around us. For example: "I hit the ball" (active) or "The ball was hit by me" (passive). Active words give us more power. For example: "Due to the increased client demand, I was forced to develop my organizational and writing skills." A more powerful, active way to say this is: "I developed my organizational skills and sharpened my professional writing abilities to better service growing client demands." This demonstrates your initiative and effort in the situation in a positive way. Two of the most powerful words in the English language are "you" and "I." The word "you" is most effective when influencing, persuading or selling to someone. The focus should be on the person we are speaking to. After all, they're not going to do something just because we think it's a good idea. They're going to respond to what they think, feel and want. Most of our statements in business should be you-based: "You're going to love this new copy machine. Imagine all the benefits to you and your company." The word "I" is best used in a conflict situation. When we are in conflict, we often begin by accusing and attacking the other person. "You were wrong. You made a mistake. You made me look bad." The other person, upon hearing this tirade of you's, begins to withdraw or becomes defensive. Either way, the communication is stopped because they are no longer listening. A more effective way to approach conflicts is to use the word "I." "I feel that there was a mistake made. I was embarrassed and felt we could have been better prepared." Nothing in that statement is directly accusing, yet you are still getting your message across and chances are the other person is still listening. The idea behind understanding which words send which messages is to make conscious decisions about the words we choose. Instead of saying things out of habit, be aware of what you say and create new, more effective habits when you speak.

Pauses are also frequently misused. An effective pause emphasizes what has just been said, or what is to come. For example, if you are going to announce a decision you have made, or a new product your company is coming out with, your speech should have pauses for dramatic emphasis. "Our company has developed a way to remove the fat content from foods. This new product, now available in test markets, will change the way the world eats (pause) – we call it 'Remove.'" This brief pause sets the audience up to hear the announcement of a new product called "Remove." Even if they were only half-listening before, when the speaker pauses, he or she recaptures their attention. They want to know what's coming after the pause. On the other hand, there are some pauses that can hurt your presentation – pauses that detract from what you are trying to say because they come at inappropriate times during your presentation – often when you have forgotten what you wanted to say or lost your place. Tag questions can have the same effect. These are questions at the end of a sentence that give the impression we are unsure of what was just said, or are looking for approval. "I know my group's solution to fighting the rumors is a good one, don't you?" The "don't you" gives that strong declarative sentence a weak ending. Think about what you really want to say and how you are going to say it. Then say exactly what you mean.

You can work to minimize the effect of power robbers on your speaking habits in three ways:
- by identifying your own tendencies
- by correcting the behavior
- by practicing to permanently replace the bad habit with a good one

The way you pronounce words can undermine your ability to influence people. Even the best-prepared, researched, written and practiced presentation will fail if you mispronounce words, use them incorrectly, or use poor diction. People who mispronounce words are thought to be poorly educated or not very bright. This is frequently untrue. Many mispronunciation problems

are the result of bad diction habits and regional pecu-
liarities. In some areas of the country, it is common to
hear the endings of words clipped off or changed, for
example: gonna for going, doin' for doing, thinkin' for
thinking, 'em for them. Most pronunciation and diction
problems can be corrected by listening to good speakers, asking when you are not sure how to pronounce a
word, looking unfamiliar words up in the dictionary or
by coaching from a qualified speech instructor.

Remember the three V's

Visual:

- Dress appropriately to help, not hinder, your
  presentation.
- Step out from behind the lectern.
- Smile when appropriate.
- Get set before starting to speak.
- Establish eye contact with audience members before
  speaking.
- Begin speaking without looking at your notes.
- Refer to your outline only occasionally.
- Don't look at the floor or out the window.
- Use gestures effectively (open palms, vary motions;
  keep them visible, smooth, natural).
- Stand up straight yet relaxed; don't lean.
- Use your facial expressions to add interest – look
  confident.
- Keep your chin up.
- Keep your feet still (no dancing, shifting or crossing
  legs). Keep your movements intentional.
- Don't pace.

- Move about, leave the podium. Get closer to your audience.
- Look like you are enjoying yourself.
- Seem to care that your audience listens. (Better yet, care).
- Appear confident and relaxed.
- Don't play with pens, pointers, visuals, hair, jewelry or rattle change in your pocket.
- Don't pack up to leave before the entire audience has left the room.

Vocal:

- Speak with enthusiasm.
- Sound interested and sincere.
- Sound spontaneous, not like you are reading or have memorized your presentation.
- Keep your pitch comfortable and low; use variation in tone.
- Keep your speaking rate at 125 to 160 words per minute. Vary the rate. Not too fast, not too slow.
- Pronounce your words carefully. Enunciate clearly.
- Use pauses for impact.
- Use voice variation (pitch, volume, rate, punch).
- Stop at the end of an idea; don't hook sentences together with "and," "and uh," or "like."
- Drop your pitch, not volume, at the end of sentences.
- Don't let your voice rise at the end of declarative sentences.
- Hide, don't emphasize, your mistakes.

Verbal:

- Use descriptive language.
- Start with a grabber to get their interest and create need.
- Use transitions to make your ideas flow.
- Use short sentences.
- Write for the ear, not the eye.
- Limit or define jargon and acronyms.
- Avoid power robbers.
- Make sure your information is interesting, useful and understandable.
- Repeat the information to enhance retention.
- Avoid words that create doubt about what you are saying ("kind of," "sort of," "I hope," "I guess," "perhaps.")
- Speak with, not at, the audience.
- Time your speech accurately.

For that perfect delivery

1. Turn off any visual aids that have been showing to focus the audience's attention solely on you. Breathe deeply, take the platform, face the audience, make eye contact and proceed with the introduction, grabber first. Movement begins only after the opening is finished.

2. Prepare for interruptions. Many interruptions can be avoided by taking simple precautions ahead of time.

- Close the doors to the presentation room.
- Post a sign warning that a presentation is in progress.
- Have an associate posted by the door to stop interruptions, when appropriate.

- Reroute or turn off any phones in the room. Put pagers on vibrate mode.
- Tell audience members when they can ask their questions.
- Let the audience know there will be a break and when it will be.

3. If you are off track, there is always the danger of departing from the planned outline and addressing subjects originally not intended as part of the presentation. Whether precipitated by an audience member's question or the speaker's desire to be as informative as possible, the result is often a loss of focus and, with it, a reduction in the presentation's effectiveness. Getting off track can often be avoided by an awareness of the danger ahead of time and a conscious effort to avoid it. This effort should be one of the motivating factors in the development of a tight outline and a final draft that can be easily referred to during the presentation. Speaking without notes should only be considered if there has been sufficient rehearsal to have the outline thoroughly learned. If, despite precautions, the presentation gets off track, use your notes to determine what was last covered, and then resume. If an audience member is involved, offer to discuss the matter later while also explaining the need to get the presentation back on track for the benefit of everyone attending. If your superior is involved, ask if the new subject should be further explored or return to what was originally planned. This last tactic most often elicits, without confrontation, a directive to return to the original presentation content.

4. If questions have followed the presentation, a second closing is needed. An indecisive ending, often consisting of a mumbled reference to the lack of more questions or time, should be avoided at all costs. You now have another opportunity to reinforce your main points and make a memorable statement.

5. Get feedback from both audience members and unbiased sources to help you improve your presentation skills. When appropriate, evaluation forms can be distributed; when not, follow-up calls to audience members can be helpful. Unobtrusive tape recorders and video cameras can be particularly helpful by showing the speaker what the audience experienced.

Practice techniques

- Practice out loud, three to six times.
- Say the presentation differently each time to keep the spontaneity.
- Practice where you will be speaking, if possible, or simulate the environment.
- Practice using your visual aids.
- Tape-record your practice. Listen, then make changes.
- Videotape your presentation, watch it, then make any necessary adjustments in content and delivery.
- Practice in front of someone similar to your audience.

Part Eight

Questions & Answers

"I'm about winning."
—**"Magic" Johnson**, played on five championship L.A. Lakers teams

The end of your presentation does not come when you finish speaking. After your summation, you still have another opportunity to face your audience members and leave them with a positive final impression. The question-and-answer period will have an impact on your audience. Do not try to escape this crucial time by sitting down or leaving the podium. This is an opportunity for you to further clarify your ideas. You don't want to give the audience the impression that you are relieved that your presentation is over and all you want to do is leave the platform. These few, simple rules will guide you through the process for a successful question-and-answer period.

- Early in your presentation, preferably as part of the introduction, tell the audience members when you will be taking questions. You may ask them to write them down to save for the end, to ask throughout your presentation, or at specific breaking points during the presentation, whichever works best for you and meets audience objectives and time allotments.

- Before answering questions, listen carefully and paraphrase the question before you respond.
- Look at the questioner while paraphrasing or include the question as part of the answer, but look at the entire audience when answering.
- Call on experts in the audience when appropriate, but take back control after they have responded.
- Set a time limit to control hostile questioners.
- Tell those with multiple questions that aren't relevant to the entire group that you will respond either at the end of the session or later to them in writing or by telephone.
- Don't let a stage hog take control.
- Don't tell a lie. If you don't know the answer to a question, say so and offer to get the information for the questioner.
- End the question-and-answer period with a strong closing remark.

How to encourage questions

It is part of your job as a presenter to encourage questions from the audience. Open up by asking, "What questions do you have?" or "Who would like to ask the first question?" In some groups, no one wants to raise a hand and go first, so you will have to make the first move. You can do this by saying, "A question I am usually asked is ... ." That should encourage others to speak up after you have answered your own question. Your position during this period should be closer to the audience. Step out from behind your lectern or table, even sit at the side of the stage if the audience will still be able to see you. Some speakers like to take questions while they stand amidst the audience. If the room setup is appropriate and you feel comfortable, it is acceptable to run the question-and-answer period this way. Pay close attention to your own body language, keeping it open and favorable. Avoid rolling your eyes, sighing or cleaning up your notes. If people are not asking questions, it means they are either bored, confused, afraid to look or sound stupid, they did not like your presentation or want to leave. If after the first question no one else volunteers one, it is appropriate to wrap up your presentation with some final words. This wrap-up can be another conclusion, you can return to your central theme, revert to your closing statement or talk about next steps. Keep your remarks brief and end with a strong finish.

How to control questions

As the presenter, it is up to you to control the question-and-answer period. Your first decision is choosing when you want to answer questions. If you are giving a training session or a sales presentation, it probably makes sense to take questions during your presentation. Don't get too far ahead of yourself. If someone asks a question that you will be covering later in your presentation, tell them so. You must also avoid a lengthy response to a question which may disturb your train of thought and the audience's ability to concentrate. You can also set aside question-and-answer periods at specified times during a presentation and announce when these will be as part of your introduction. This gives your audience members the chance to formulate their questions during your presentation.

How to handle hostility

As a presenter, you may find yourself facing a hostile questioner. Your skill at disarming verbal attacks will reflect on your credibility with audience members and the impression they have of both you and your presentation. The following approach works well to diffuse hostile questioners:

- Let them say whatever they want to. You listen while they vent.
- Paraphrase what they have just said, and how they feel about it, without being condescending.
- Ask probing questions to try to find out what the real issues are.
- Choose one of the following options:
  "I know what your issues are, now let me respond."
  "Let's problem-solve together to work this out."
  "Let's look into this after this presentation has concluded."

By using this approach, you have indicated that you value the thoughts and feelings of the questioner. The audience will respect you, and you will diffuse the hostility at the same time.

How to respond to questions

When You Know The Answer: A good way to begin

when you know the answer is to paraphrase the question or include it as part of the answer. This clarifies the fact that you understand the question and have heard it correctly. Then answer it. Avoid the tendency to say, "That's a good question" before you answer, or "Did I answer your question?" after you have responded. When you compliment one questioner, it becomes awkward if you don't compliment the next questioner, and so on. If you have asked, "Did I answer your question?" and the answer is negative, you have destroyed some of your credibility with the audience. You also run the risk of embarrassing the questioner if he or she doesn't understand your answer. A good way to make sure you have answered the question is to ask the same questioner if he or she has any other questions for you, or if they would like more explanation. When you do know the answer, keep your answer short and interesting to most of the group (long answers discourage more questions). If the question isn't relevant to most people, tell the questioner that you will meet with him or her after the presentation. If the decision maker is asking the question, take the time to answer it.

When you don't know the answer to a question, be truthful. Simply say, "I don't have the answer," or "I don't have that information," and you can offer to get the information and get back to that person at a later time. Ask the person to give you his or her card with the question on it, or write it down yourself with the person's phone number. You also can offer them a source for the information, or you can open it up to the audience or an expert in the group who may know the answer. Don't dwell on it, keep the question-and-answer session moving. Do anticipate the questions in advance and prepare answers. Don't make up answers.

If you encounter a stage hog who persists in asking you one question after another, you will need to make a decision. If the questions are relevant to the topic and merit consideration, answer them, but after a few questions, nicely say it's time to give someone else a turn. If the questions are not relevant, answer the first question or two and then cut him or her short. If you have identified a potential stage hog prior to your presentation, try meeting with the person in advance to discuss his or her ideas. Mention any that have merit during your presentation; that will make this person feel good and probably save you from disruption during your question-and-answer period.

Ending with a strong finish

When your presentation is over, and the questions have stopped, or time is up, it's time to conclude. Don't make the mistake of giving a simple "thank you" and leaving the podium. This is your last chance to leave a positive impression on the audience. Return to the central theme, revert to your closing statement or talk about next steps. Your closing should not be lengthy, but it should wrap things up neatly. An example of a closing might be: "We've learned how and why Vest-A-Cop programs work, now it is up to us to make our police officers and our citizens safer."

Final thoughts on questions & answers

- Tell audience members when you will be taking questions and whether there is a limit on the number they can ask.
- Encourage questions by having an open body stance and personal enthusiasm.
- Ask a question yourself, if necessary.
- Listen carefully and paraphrase questions before responding.
- Look at the questioner when paraphrasing a question; look at the entire audience when responding.
- If you don't know the answer, say so. Offer to get back to the questioner either in writing or by phone, at a later date.
- Don't let a stage hog take control.
- Handle hostile questioners with tact and diplomacy, but cut them short.
- Respect the questioner and don't be defensive.
- Keep your answers brief.
- End the question-and-answer session with a memorable closing statement.

Part Nine
Special Types Of Presentations

"When you go to the Olympic Games, you're taking on the rest of the world, in front of the entire world."
– **Bruce Jenner,** Olympic gold medalist

Many of the opportunities you will have to make presentations throughout your career will involve other speakers. These occasions may take the form of panel discussions, symposiums, forums and other group situations. To be effective, team presentations must be meticulously planned and executed and well-coordinated, like a ballet where each dancer knows exactly where to stand, when to move and when to exit from the stage. The stakes are often high, as in the award of advertising contracts where millions of dollars ride on the presentation dynamics of one advertising agency team vs. a team from another agency – often with the same levels of experience and creativity. What makes one team stand out? If the team works like a smooth, well-oiled machine, if one member's presentation flows into the next presentation, and if all members present themselves professionally and intelligently, the impression left is one of confidence and competence. Team presentations come with their own unique set of problems. For a single presenter, developing a well-crafted and executed presentation falls on his or her shoulders alone. But as part of a group, there is the added constraint of worrying about the rest of the team. Decisions have to be made in concert with the other team members, and this can lead to confusion and controversy. It is therefore essential to have one strong team leader who will guide and coordinate members' presentations, making sure each person has his or her area covered adequately and ensuring that one member's presentation does not duplicate someone else's.

Six steps to a successful team presentation

1. Pick the right leader. Often the person with seniority is automatically designated team leader. This may not work if that person is busy with other projects or has too much day-to-day responsibility to spend the time necessary coordinating all members' presentations. The team leader should possess the most knowledge of the topic or client, and be one who the other members respect and someone they know is objective and will give them fair criticism.

2. Agreement on the focus. Each member of the team should be aware that his or her contribution is essential to the success of the presentation, and no one member's part is more important than another's.

3. Frequent updates and review of material. All team members should be discussing their part of the presentation with the team leader to ensure they are headed in the right direction. Group meetings should be held so everyone is aware of where the other members are heading.

4. Proper audience analysis. Team presentations are usually given to other teams. This means the audience members may come from different levels in their organization, from different departments and have different agendas of their own. Each member of the presenting team should understand who the audience is and consider its knowledge levels and interests.

5. Pay attention to details. The leader or a designate should have responsibility for the details such as room arrangements, equipment, visual aids and handouts. Everything in a team presentation should be coordinated and reviewed well in advance of presentation day. If possible, this person should also arrange for team members to practice in the room where they will be presenting.

6. Mutual respect for team members. The group dynamics will be apparent to the audience. A team that works well together, respects each other's part in the presentation and enjoys being together will have the advantage. If your team is made up of people from different departments who may not have had the chance to meet, schedule an informal lunch or dinner so they can get to know each other. The comfort level team members have with each other will help them to relax and do their best during the presentation.

If you are the team leader

If you are the team leader, much of the planning and details will be your responsibility. The other members of the team will be looking to you for guidance and validation that their presentations will be effective. To ensure the best for your team, your responsibilities should include the following:

- Buy-in of the concepts and strategies from management. It is up to you to schedule a meeting with key people before the team begins working. This will avoid having to do things over again later if management doesn't agree with the direction you have taken. The support of management will be important to team members and will help to encourage them.

- Audience analysis. As team leader, you should be prepared to gather information on the audience. If another member of the team has more contact with the audience, assign that person the job of preparing the audience analysis. This information should include the key players and decision makers in the audience.

- Define the strategy for your team. You have met with management and mapped out a strategy for the presentation. It is up to you to meet with your team and make sure each member is comfortable with the strategy. It is also up to you to give a clear picture of the audience and marketing strategy to those members of the team who may lack insight into these areas.

- Assign the topics. If you have chosen your team or had them assigned to you, as leader you will most likely be assigning each presenter his or her topic. In creative presentations, writers and art directors know what their areas are, but it is still up to the leader to explain what each member of the team is expected to do.

- Make a schedule. You should schedule time for individual meetings with each presenter and for the group to meet for run-throughs and updates. This will give team members the chance to familiarize themselves with each other's work, and to see how the presentation fits together.

- Provide strong leadership and direction. The team members will be looking to you to make sure everything is on track. It is up to you to stay on schedule, on budget and on course. Failing to provide strong leadership may result in missed deadlines, extensive rework and an unhappy team. This will lead to poor performance.

If you are the moderator of a panel discussion

- It is your responsibility to introduce the topic to be discussed and each speaker. It should have been decided beforehand if the moderator will list the panelists' credentials or if each panelist will give a brief self-introduction.
- You will be opening and closing each segment of the discussion. It will also be your responsibility to maintain proper timing to give each panelist a fair share of the time. The moderator keeps track of how long each speaker has to make his or her point and warns when time is running out. If the speaker keeps going over the allotted time, it is up to the moderator to stop the presentation.
- The moderator will also provide a bridge between speech segments and may or may not comment between presenters. He or she may simply move the discussion along if comments are not appropriate.

The moderator opens the question-and-answer session, paraphrases the questions and calls on the person who will respond. At the end of the question-and-answer period, it is the moderator's responsibility to end the discussion and conclude.

Meetings that work

Many of the presentations you will give throughout your business career will be at meetings. On average, executives spend more than 50 percent of their time at meetings. Whether or not that time is well-spent is the question. If you are the person calling the meeting, be sure to ask yourself the question, "Is a meeting really necessary?" before you schedule one. Clearly understanding the objectives will help you to determine if a meeting is needed. What is your desired end result? Is there an alternative to a meeting that will be just as effective? What are the alternatives? Once your objectives are known it becomes easier to decide the best way to achieve them. A meeting may be the only answer, but phone calls, e-mail or memos might be just as effective.

If you are asked by someone else to arrange a meeting, your first task is to answer the question, "What is the purpose?" It may be:

- To solve a problem
- To share information
- To plan a strategy
- To gather information
- To provide instruction

- To showcase someone's abilities
- To brainstorm ideas
- To review data

When a meeting is planned without thought to its purpose, the attendees often arrive with competing or conflicting perceptions of why they are there. It is advised that an agenda or memo defining the purpose of the meeting be distributed to all invitees prior to scheduling the meeting. This way, if there is another way to accomplish the purpose, or an alternative method of dealing with it, you will find out in advance.

If a meeting is needed, who should attend? The purpose of the meeting should determine who needs to be there. In large corporations, representatives from various divisions may be needed; in a small organization, only a decision maker and one or two others may be sufficient. In selecting who to invite to the meeting, your objectives as a presenter should be considered. If you are not the organizer but have been asked to present, there may be someone in the organization you want to hear your presentation — either because it affects him or her directly, or because you want this person to see you in action. Request that this person be invited and let the organizer know why.

Successful meetings require careful planning. If you will be creating the agenda, how should you present the information? Agendas should be brief and to the point. You could use phrasing in the form of questions, accompanied by a brief statement of justification for including the item on the agenda. If an agenda is covering only one topic and various participants will be presenting segments, use the purpose as the meeting title, and include each participant's segment, name, department and position. It also is important to include a timetable.

When scheduling a meeting, it is your responsibility to make sure the basic requirements for the meeting room are arranged.

- Is the room large enough for the number of attendees?
- Is there adequate light and air?
- Is the room isolated from outside interruptions?
- Is the room convenient for attendees?
- Is the room available for the time you have scheduled?
- Is there adequate seating?
- If you will be using audio/visual/computer equipment, will it be supplied and is the room properly wired?
- Use the following worksheet to help you.

Meeting planning worksheet

1. **Objectives:** What are the desired results of this meeting?

2. **Time:** How long will it last? When should it be held?

3. Attendees: Who needs to be there? Are decision makers, information presenters and information gatherers included?

4. Agenda: What is the schedule of events? Who is involved in preparing and distributing the agenda?

5. Physical Arrangements: What kind of facilities and equipment are needed? What are the specific room arrangements?

6. Evaluations: How will the meeting be evaluated?

Brody
COMMUNICATIONS LTD.

P.O. Box 8868 • Elkins Park, PA 19027 • Phone: 215-886-1688 • Fax: 215-886-1699
E-mail: brodycomm@brodycomm.com • http://www.brodycomm.com

AGENDA

Group Name: _____   Date: _____

Meeting Objectives: _____   Starting Time: _____

Called by: _____   Ending Time: _____

Meeting Type: _____   Breaks: _____

Background Materials: _____   Place: _____

Please Bring: _____

_____   Decision Making Method: _____

_____   _____

Leader: _____   Final Decision Maker: _____

_____   _____

Recorder: _____   Special Notes: _____

Facilitator: _____   _____

Participants: _____   _____

_____   _____

_____   _____

AGENDA	PERSON RESPONSIBLE	TIME ALLOTTED

During the meeting planning stage you will need to prepare an agenda. Prior to issuing the actual agenda, survey the proposed participants to find out their needs and concerns so that the final agenda is planned with those needs in mind. This is also a way to surface hidden agendas. A brief memo may be distributed to accomplish this, and can include the following three questions:

1. What topics would you like to present during our meeting on _____?
2. How much time will you need to present?
3. What issues or concerns would you like to be discussed?

You will then be able to plan and distribute your agenda prior to the meeting. On the day of the meeting bring enough agendas along to distribute to participants along with any background materials, charts, markers, pads, pens, flip charts, etc., that may not be supplied for you. If you will be leading the meeting, you will have 10 basic responsibilities:

1. Start the meeting promptly. Call or have someone else call any latecomers.
2. State the objectives.
3. Follow the agenda.
4. Manage the flow.
5. Facilitate discussion.
6. Deal with problems/difficult participants.
7. Help to resolve conflicts.
8. Clarify next steps/action plan.
9. Summarize.

10. Evaluate.

As a meeting leader, you may be faced with handling difficult participants. These usually fall into one or more of five categories: overly dominating, rambling, side conversationalists, non-contributors and negative participants. Here are some suggestions for dealing with these problems:

Overly dominating: Credit the person's knowledge of the subject and any constructive contributions. State the need for others to be heard. Ask the group for reactions. Intervene in personal attacks by partially paraphrasing informational content of the attack, if there is any. If the participant is out of line, acknowledge his or her feelings and move on.

Rambling: Wait for a break or pause and intervene. Confirm your understanding of the basic points. Restate the urgency of time constraints. Direct a question to another participant or the group and refocus or restate the objectives.

Side conversationalists: Stop speaking and look at the talkers. Ask them if they have any questions. Restate objectives and ask them to hold side conversations until the meeting has ended. Lower your volume and speak more toward them. Avoid embarrassing people.

Non-contributors: You don't want to embarrass them but you could try to get these types involved through direct questions. Talk to non-contributors at break time to find out why they are quiet. Give them specific responsibilities.

Negative participants: Find out if the negative feelings are shared by the group. Ask the negative person to record the minutes; this keeps him or her busy and less able to speak out. Talk to this person individually at break time to try to uncover the reason for the negativity.

Evaluating the meeting

Meetings should be evaluated in two ways: by the meeting leader and by the participants. In small, informal meetings, an evaluation can take place at the close of the meeting during the summation or final remarks of the meeting leader. For larger meetings, the following personal evaluation forms can help you to clarify whether the meeting met its objectives and gather the participants' feelings.

Personal evaluation for meeting leaders

- Was this meeting necessary?
- Were my objectives clear?
- Was my agenda organized and distributed before the meeting?
- Did I invite only/all necessary participants?
- Did I arrive early and check on the room arrangements and the equipment?
- Did the meeting begin/end on time?
- Was the agenda followed?
- Did I stay within allotted time frames?
- Did I encourage participation?
- Did I effectively resolve conflicts?
- Did I maintain control?

- Were the final decisions summarized and action plan outlined?
- Did I follow up by sending minutes to participants?
- Was there an evaluation?
- Was follow-up action done by the participants?

Personal evaluation for meeting participants

- Was the purpose of the meeting clear to me?
- Did I understand my role?
- Did I prepare my information well?
- Was I on time?
- Did I conduct side conversations during the meeting?
- Did I ask pertinent/relevant questions?
- Was I open to the ideas of others?
- Was I a good listener?
- Did I participate as fully as possible?
- Did I help to facilitate/maintain discussion?
- Did I complete the follow-up action?
- Did I evaluate the meeting and give helpful feedback?

Closing the meeting

The meeting leader should be the one who ends the meeting. It is best to give a five- or 10-minute warning, giving group members time to finish their remarks. If the meeting has fallen behind and some items on the agenda cannot be completed, the leader must indicate these and propose an alternative time or method for including them. As leader, responsibilities include:

Summarizing the conclusions and stating:
- how the meeting was useful

- the objectives that were achieved
- the next steps to be taken
- areas of responsibility

Thanking the group by:

- expressing appreciation for everyone's participation
- giving credit to individuals

If an additional meeting of the same group has been scheduled, the leader should include this in the closing remarks.

Videoconferences

While telephones, computers and the written word are still the primary methods of business communication, the video age has taken us much further in our ability to communicate face-to-face. It is so much better to see the person we are dealing with, whether that person is across town or on the other side of the globe. With videoconferencing joining other mainstream methods of communication, we can be face-to-face with anyone, anywhere in the world. Many corporations of today have their own videoconferencing facility, with in-house staff to make it work smoothly. But you don't have to work for a large corporation to take advantage of videoconferencing. Many rental facilities exist, staffed by experts who can guide you step-by-step through the process.

The capability to link two or more locations almost anywhere in the world makes videoconferencing valuable for companies doing business globally. Giving a presentation over a videoconferencing network is very different from presenting to a live audience. Imagine yourself projected onto the screen of your computer. How will you look and sound? You will probably be seated, facing a camera, and a video screen will show people on the other end of the conference. They will be in a similar setup. You will probably appear primarily as a talking head. Your visual aids will be presented through another camera, leading to confusion if you have not carefully choreographed with the camera operator when to show them. Find out in advance if you will be able to stand or show the visuals yourself. When preparing your presentation, keep the camera setup in mind. If you are unsure of how to prepare, meet in advance with the program facilitator who may be able to show you a sample of an actual videoconference or demonstrate how it will work.

Tips for videoconferences

• **Size counts:** Videoconferences are best suited to small, geographically dispersed groups. With large groups, it is difficult to see the other participants.

• **Have a backup plan if things malfunction.** Consider an audio conference if the video fails.

• **Make proper introductions.** Once connected, let the other site know that you are there. It can be embarrassing to see and overhear something that was not intended for everyone. As with any meeting, introductions should be made while making sure each participant is visible when making his or her introduction.

• **Establish a facilitator.** This person will run the meeting and make sure the agenda is followed. He or she will also make opening and closing remarks.

• **Watch the remote locations.** When the room is equipped with monitors for both the remote and local sites, don't watch yourself on the monitor during the conference. Remember that the other side is watching you: You don't want to be viewed checking your hair or makeup or doing anything unsightly. Focus your attention on the person speaking.

• **Pay attention to grooming.** The video camera magnifies you. What you wear and how you are groomed is going to be noticed. Visualize yourself projected on a big screen television; anything out of place is going to show up. It is best to avoid checks, plaids and overly bright colors.

• **Show consideration for others.** Speak in a normal tone of voice; it's not necessary to shout to be heard. Most videoconferencing systems produce a slight delay of audio between sites. As a result, it is important to wait until the person speaking is finished before commenting. Talking over someone else will cause confusion – and it's rude.

Videoconference practice:

• Prepare a five-minute presentation (subject doesn't matter) and videotape yourself. Watch the tape several times and give yourself an honest critique. Then tape yourself again and do the same thing. If you keep repeating the same mistakes, concentrate on improving them when you videotape yourself again. If you find yourself using power robbers while speaking (umm's, ah's, like, you know) keep practicing until you can speak smoothly for five minutes without using any. Then videotape yourself again. You may have to do this five or six times before you feel comfortable in front of the camera. If you are unhappy with how you look or your facial expressions, practice speaking in front of a mirror until you have eliminated the unwanted expressions. Then, videotape yourself again.

• If you find yourself terrified of the camera, remember, being comfortable is not something that comes naturally to many people. Even seasoned broadcasters admit to recurring stage fright. A series of relaxation exercises like the ones in chapter six may help you to feel more in control.

• If you don't like the way you look on camera, remember that what you have to say is going to be more important than how you look. However, this is the time for a natural hairstyle and natural makeup. Although the lights may make you look washed out, you don't want to look like you're going on the stage. A little more blush for women is usually all that's necessary. For men who perspire and shine when nervous, a light dusting of cornstarch with a large brush on the nose, forehead and chin can eliminate that shiny look.

• What you wear can distract from what you have to say. For those on the other end of your videoconference, who may never have seen you before, this is going to be their only impression of you. Choose subdued or neutral colors appropriate to your style and coloring. Suggest.

Avoid bright, flashy colors. Men should avoid loud ties. Simple jewelry is appropriate; avoid dangling or jangling earrings, bracelets or necklaces. For men, avoid ties with narrow, repeating stripes which can be distracting on camera. If you wear glasses, select those with non-glare lenses and rims. Depending on how the room is lit, they may cause a glare.

Part Ten

Special Occasion Presentations

"I do not try to be better than anybody else. I only try to be better than myself."
– **Dan Jansen,** Olympic gold medalist

Special occasions

In the course of your career, you will probably find yourself called upon to speak at a special occasion. Unlike making an informative or persuasive presentation, often the goal of speaking at a special occasion is to be inspirational or motivational, so choosing the right words and coming across to your audience as sincere are essential. Using colorful language will help you to express your thoughts about the occasion. Your words should arouse emotion and focus the audience's thoughts and feelings on who or what is being honored or commemorated. If you read your speech from note cards, you will not seem sincere, therefore, it is essential that you know your key points and introduction cold.

When speaking at a special occasion, your technique and organizational skills are less important than at other kinds of presentations because there are clear expectations of what your speech should contain. For

example: If you are honoring a recently promoted executive, the audience will expect to hear about his or her
accomplishments and awards, possibly a humorous
anecdote about the person, and perhaps that person's
new or future responsibilities within the company. If
you are presenting at a roast, you would expect to be
telling stories at the honoree's expense. All in fun and
good taste, of course.

Some speakers prefer to start their speeches with a joke.
Jokes can grab an audience's attention, but unless you
are extremely comfortable using humor and are positive
that your humor will be appreciated – and that it is
really funny – you should not tell jokes when asked to
speak at a special occasion. That does not mean you
won't be able to use humor, it simply means that jokes
are best left to professionals.

When you are asked to speak at a special occasion, it
may be to introduce other speakers, speak at testimoni-
als, banquets or ceremonials, or deliver welcome or exit
speeches, perhaps even a eulogy. It is important for you
to understand what is expected of you, and for you to
perform accordingly.

Welcome presentation

The welcome presentation is designed to welcome people
into companies or organizations, or groups to events, and
is generally a short speech used to begin an event or occasion. This type of presentation sets the mood and flow of

upcoming events and outlines the occasion for the audience so they know what to expect. The expectation is to associate the values of the welcoming group with those values possessed by the person being welcomed.

Example: "Good morning associates, family and friends. The board of directors and I would like to welcome you to our first annual employee and family day. Today will give all of you, and all of us, the opportunity to learn about each other and our families as we join in games and activities designed to further the goals of our company."

Welcome speeches are also used to begin occasions such as wedding receptions, awards banquets and dinner receptions, and they tend to have a strong impact on the audience. It gives the event organizers, hosts or sponsors an opportunity to show who they are and what the event is about, and will set the tone. The welcome speech is an opportunity for you to distinguish yourself. If you do a good job welcoming your boss to his or her anniversary dinner, you may find yourself asked to give more presentations in the future.

Speeches of introduction

A strong introduction should generate enthusiasm and give audience members a quick overview of the person they are about to encounter. It should include accurate information and enhance the impression of the person about to make his or her way to the platform. A good introduction generates excitement and enthusiasm for the upcoming speaker or performer, and makes the audience receptive to what is going to be said or done.

Example: "Marjorie Brody has a secret. This secret has led her from the quiet life of a college professor to the platform of some of the world's most prestigious organizations. Marjorie knows the secret of using personal marketing to make life-changing events happen. Today, she is going to share that secret with you, and then you will be able to change your life as well."

An introduction that detracts something from the person being presented or his or her presentation can ruin the entire event. Be careful not to give misleading, useless, speculative or untrue information. Finally, be sure you pronounce the person's name correctly. When in doubt, ask for the correct pronunciation before you go out in front of an audience, and write it out phonetically. If you are being introduced, it is a good idea to write your own introduction and send it in advance to the person doing the introduction. Bring an extra copy to the event.

Acceptance speeches

You've just won "Employee of the Year" at your company, and during the luncheon in your honor you will be making an acceptance speech. This isn't the Academy Awards, and it's also not the time to be dramatic. Be sincere and let your thanks be heartfelt. Thank the person or persons giving you the award, and anyone who inspired or helped you, including your family. A gracious and sincere acceptance speech will be remembered, and you will be seen in a positive light. Acceptance speeches are common in the world of business, politics and entertainment.

Example: "I feel like I have grown up at Brody Communications. And it's been a wonderful experience for me. Today, you are honoring me by naming me "Employee of the Year" – but I would also like to honor you. Having the opportunity to be a part of a company like Brody Communications has taught me about the important things in a career – the opportunity to grow, to experience loyalty, to develop my skills and to be appreciated for them. To my co-workers and to those who granted me this honor today, I say, "Thank you."

Inauguration speech

The inauguration speech is usually given by a person who is assuming the head of an organization or government. This can include speeches delivered by the incoming president of a club or the president of an association. The objectives in this type of presentation are to reaffirm the values of the organization you are about to head and to state the goals you will attempt to achieve while in that position.

Some goals to keep in mind: Note the accomplishments of your predecessor; highlight your own accomplishments without bragging; include the direction you and your team would like to take; make everyone there want to be on your team.

Eulogies

If you are asked to say a few words about someone you have worked with (or for) keep your remarks short and tactful. Although you and Jim might have had some great times after work at the corner pub, this is not the time to mention them. Be respectful of the family.

Example: "Jim and I spent the past 15 years working side by side at Plaza Computers. He was a thoughtful co-worker and good friend. I will miss sharing ideas with him and learning from Jim ... ."

The toastmaster or master of ceremonies

This is the person who conducts the event. This type of an occasion can be a company dinner, retirement party, roast, birthday or even an event for visiting delegations of some kind (students, politicians, foreign visitors, etc.). It is the responsibility of the toastmaster to play a leading part in running the show. He or she makes sure everything goes smoothly and stays on time, and also plays a part as master of ceremonies or moderator. The toastmaster gives the opening remarks, leads the group into the meal (if applicable), introduces other speakers and closes the event. If awards are to be handed out, the toastmaster may perform that role as well, or introduce those who will be doing it. If there is to be a question-and-answer period, it is also the job of the toastmaster to facilitate this. The toastmaster should communicate in advance with other speakers to make certain procedures are clear and to assign time slots. If things drag, the toastmaster should tactfully step in or alert the speaker that time is running out. It is also up to the toastmaster to avoid putting anyone on the spot who does not wish to speak. This is especially true during ceremonies where those honored are surprised and may not wish to speak.

New employee orientations

These events are often coordinated by the human resources department in large companies. As part of an orientation program, you may be asked to speak to a group of new employees or trainees. Get specific information as to what is expected of you, who else will be speaking and the topics they will be covering, and the amount of time you have for your presentation. You will be giving the new employees information about your area of expertise, and your presentation should take into account the limited amount of knowledge they may have about how things work at the company. This is an occasion to provide information and to generate a positive impression of yourself and your department. As you will probably be presenting as part of a group, respect the time constraints. If there will not be enough time to answer questions, offer new employees a best method or time to contact you for additional information. If you will be representing your department, check with others you work with to see if they would like you to include any information you may not have thought of.

The farewell speech

These speeches are commonplace today as people change jobs, and careers, frequently. If you will be speaking on your own departure, mention some of the memorable experiences you shared with the people there and indicate how these experiences have contributed to your growth and enjoyment. It's a time you can single out people who made a significant contribution to your work experience and thank them. If you are speaking about someone else who is leaving, pay tribute to him or her by recognizing that person's contributions to the company.

Using stories & anecdotes

When a businessperson is asked to speak at a special occasion, you are not expected to be the entertainment. But you can use humor naturally by telling your own stories and anecdotes. It is a good idea for you to compile a collection of your own humorous stories or others you have heard that you will feel comfortable sharing with the audience. An advantage of telling your own stories is that they help to build rapport with the audience. This is true with co-workers and employees who will see you in a new light as you share a part of yourself with them. If the stories are work related and you all work in the same company or industry, there will be a unique feeling of relating — you to the audience members and they to you as you share in your story. Your own stories need not be strictly work related. You can use humorous anecdotes from your own life, for example:

- trips you have taken
- your family
- your childhood
- your own career path
- your hobbies
- your friends
- your own embarrassing moments
- your fears

By sharing your own personal stories, you will quickly make a connection with listeners, and they will be more receptive to whatever comes next in your presentation. A word of caution: If you are delivering a special occasion speech that is negative, like company downsizing or a reduction in stock price, this is not the time to begin with a humorous anecdote.

Part Eleven

Meet The Pros

"I want to be remembered as a person who felt there was no limitation to what the human body and mind can do, and be the inspiration to lead people to do things they never hoped to do."
– **Carl Lewis**, Olympic track and field star, winner of nine gold medals, one silver medal.

One of the most beneficial things I do for myself as a professional speaker is observe other professional speakers at work and solicit their opinions about relevant subjects. To give you the benefit of other speakers' knowledge and experience, I have asked 10 top speaking professionals to share with you their own methods and tips for success in a variety of situations. Their phone numbers are included if you would like to contact them directly.

Ten Tips For Presenting Technical Material To Management Audiences

by William R. Steele

When conducting a course on presentation skills, it's common to have participants ask about the challenge of presenting technical material to non-technical audiences. Their biggest concern is with presentations given to "management."

To hear the management people talk, this concern is

well-founded. Technical presentations often frustrate them. Time and again, they find themselves on the receiving end of a "data dump," buried in technical jargon instead of enlightened.

When a technical presenter faces a management audience, it's like the meeting of two different worlds. Language, context, knowledge base and priorities can all be different. The successful technical presenter steps over into the audience's world, and gives an audience-centered presentation. The presenter becomes an interpreter who translates the technical message for audience members, making sure their needs drive the process.

Here are 10 tips that can help any technical presenter develop this ability:

1. Less is more. It's not how much information you give out that counts, but how much the audience comprehends and retains. The all-important question is, "What did they walk away with?"

Ironically, with non-technical audiences, the transfer of knowledge is often in direct inverse proportion to the amount of technical detail given. Management finds it difficult to digest a detail-heavy presentation that, for an audience of fellow technical experts, might be just right.

Management wants the essential information needed to make an overall assessment and subsequent decisions. Have the back-up science, engineering and math available, but don't automatically include all these details in your presentation.

2. Don't forget: It's a jungle to them. When presenting technical information, it's easy to forget that the management audience's familiarity with it is likely to be less than yours – less in-depth. You have been immersed in the subject; they have not.

Preview. Provide multiple internal summaries. Review. You are a tour guide; don't charge through this "jungle" of information and lose the audience along the way.

3. Don't assume they understand. It is reasonable to assume that people who have made it into upper-level management are smart. What is not reasonable to assume is that these people will instantly understand all the technical concepts included in your presentation – or that they will say something if they don't.

Assume that your audience will benefit from extra efforts to make things understandable. An extra example, analogy or rephrased explanation helps more often than it hurts. Your audience is more likely to become frustrated by a lack of understanding than impatient with your extra efforts.

4. Keep referring back to what they already know. Understanding and memory are based on association. You can improve both for your audience members by relating new material back to what they already know. Highlight similarities; point out notable differences.

Note: When a management decision is needed, consider referring to similar or related decisions made in the past. Such references can not only help with understanding, they can increase comfort with the requested decision.

5. Use visuals and simplify. The old saying "A picture is worth a thousand words" certainly holds true with technical presentations. With visuals, comprehension not only improves, it speeds up (no small consideration given the notorious impatience of management).

Keep in mind, however, the "picture" that's worth "a thousand words" is just that – a picture. It's not paragraphs from a script, or your notes in bullet-point form, projected on the screen primarily to help you. A visual is most effective when it is a graphical (i.e. pictorial) representation.

Also, simplicity is essential. If management's quick comprehension is the objective, complexity is the enemy. If something is unavoidably complex, consider a building process over several visuals.

6. Hold "lingo" to the necessary minimum. Spend enough time in a technical specialty and you will end up speaking a language few people outside that specialty can understand. Loaded with lingo, buzzwords, jargon, technical terms and acronyms, this language will become second nature, so familiar its use is unconscious.

Strive to speak in a language that everyone in your

audience will understand. If possible, preview your presentation with someone outside your specialty who can point out language problems you may have missed.

When technical terms are unavoidable, and using acronyms makes sense for convenience, explain them when they first come up. If there are many of them, consider providing a reference key on a flip chart or in a handout.

7. Welcome interaction and adapt. Management audiences will often interrupt presentations with comments, questions and discussions. For the presenter set on getting through complex technical material, this can be frustrating. The tendency is to doggedly plow on as opportunities to speak present themselves.

Instead of viewing audience involvement as something to struggle with, plan for it and make use of this participation. Prepare a flexible presentation that does not require all the time allotted. Then, since you are freed of time pressures, listen for the valuable feedback audience involvement provides. Do listeners understand the material? What needs to be re-explained? What can be skipped? What priorities are audience members revealing?

Getting through your prepared material, despite interruptions, does not define success – effectively responding to the needs and desires of the audience does.

8. Demonstrate. When possible, take a step beyond verbal descriptions and pictures; actually demonstrate what you are talking about. The impact on the audience can be dramatic, increasing both comprehension and memorability.

Keep in mind, however, passing things around the room for close inspection is not a good idea during your presentation. Audience members will inevitably pay more attention to what is being passed around than to you. Although management types may ask to see items right away – and their wishes cannot be ignored – it's best to promise opportunities for later inspection.

9. Do the unexpected. Management audiences will often walk into a technical presentation with a "here we go again" cynicism. The speaker faces distracted, inattentive, impatient people.

Part of the problem is the boilerplate nature of so many technical presentations. In the name of protocol, they slavishly follow a long-established formula. No one can remember when this formula was originally adopted – or why. What in all likelihood is an old-fashioned rut is either unconsciously followed or rationalized as the "proper/approved/standard" way these presentations have always been done.

You are only going to succeed if you capture your audience's attention. This is going to be hard if your presentation is indistinguishable from the hundreds that have preceded it.

While being sensitive to what is officially required, look for opportunities to do something new, different, unexpected. It doesn't have to be radical, just imaginative enough to pique some interest.

10. Sell! Ask a room full of technical presenters how many are in sales and few, if any, hands will go up. In truth, everybody is in sales.

Stressing benefits is the essence of sales. Convincing audience members they will benefit from what is being presented is the key to holding their attention.

Do not assume that the value of what you are saying is self-evident. Point out the value. Point out the benefits. Point out the possibilities. If your audience members don't desire the information you are providing (i.e. are not being "sold" on its value), they are not going to try to absorb it. If you want to be more successful making technical presentations to non-technical, management audiences, keep these 10 tips in mind. They'll help you bridge the communication gap. And, remember, the key to all effective communication is being tuned into your audience.

William R. Steele is a senior training associate at Brody Communications Ltd. He has been a senior vice president at a large advertising agency and is a widely published technical writer. Bill can be contacted at 215-886-1688 or by e-mail at brodycomm@brodycomm.com

Why Use Humor In A Presentation?

by Tom Antion

"Why should I bother using humor in my presentations? Can't I just deliver my information and sit down?" Yes, you sure can, and that's what most people do. The problem is that most people are not effective presenters. They are snooze-inducing, say-your-prayers, hit-the-sack, unlicensed hypnotists. They might be experts in their fields and be able to recite hours and hours of information on their topics, but is that effective? No. An effective presentation is one that achieves its purpose, whatever that may be.

I don't think that many presenters define their purpose clearly even to themselves. As part of being a strong presenter you must ask yourself: Why am I here? What do I want to accomplish? Am I here to sell something? Am I here to motivate? Am I here to persuade? Am I here to get votes? What do I want the audience members to take home with them when I'm done? Once you've answered these questions, I can tell you how and why humor can help you achieve your goals.

According to Bob Orben, special assistant to President Gerald Ford and former director of the White House speech writing department, "Business executives and political leaders have embraced humor because humor works. Humor has gone from being an admirable part of a leader's character to a mandatory one."

There is a higher level of professional speaker to progress to, and developing outstanding presentation skills will help you become that person.

A survey conducted by a large executive search firm of top executives who earned more than $250,000 per year found that these executives believed their communication skills were the number one factor that carried them to the top. Mastering the use of humor and other high-explosion techniques puts a fine polish on those skills, which can help propel you to the top more quickly.

Like other top presenters, there are many benefits you can derive from using humor in your presentations. Keep in mind that these benefits only help you reach your ultimate purpose for making the presentation. They are not purposes themselves unless, of course, you are only interested in entertaining.

Using humor does the following for you:

Helps you connect with the audience. What audience members are going to listen to you if they don't feel you are one of them?

Makes you more likeable. The more audience members like you, the more they will be likely to agree with your ideas.

Arouses interest. Many of you speak to people who don't even want to be there. Humor can help you gain their interest.

Keeps attention. Grabbing interest at the beginning of a presentation is not enough to carry you to the end. You must keep the audience's attention all the way. Unfortunately our audience's attention spans are becoming shorter and shorter. According to Ron Hoff in his presentation skills book *I Can See You Naked,* "If corporate managers ever saw their own meetings on TV, they would pick up their remote controls and zap themselves into oblivion in the flick of an eyelash." We are competing with movies that have $100 million in special effects. We must be prepared to deliver a fast-paced program that surprises members of the audience. At times we need to quickly capture their attention and make sure they are listening to us. Humor will help you do this.

Helps to emphasize points and ideas. Anyone who has ever taken a basic speech course knows that you must hit audience members on the head with your point over and over before they get it. Humor is one of the hammers you can use.

Disarms hostility. Non-frivolous humor can be used to take the edge off audiences that are clearly against you.

Reduces relative status. Some of you are what I call the "big-shots" of your organizations. Your position as boss creates a big barrier to listening. Making a little fun of yourself (self-effacing humor) will do wonders for opening the lines of communication.

Overcomes overly flattering introductions.
Introducers come in all levels of quality. If you get one that makes you sound too good to be true, it will create expectations in the audience that you couldn't possibly live up to. Humor can neutralize this problem instantly.

Gets your point across without creating hostility.
Sometimes you have to deliver tough negative messages. The careful use of humor can help you do your dastardly deed without creating unnecessary anger.

Helps relate facts and figures. A friend of mine likes to say, "I don't want to bore you with sadistics." Technical and financial presenters must be especially careful to spice up long lists of numbers and generally dry material. You must keep in mind that most people in your audience are not as passionate about your subject as you are or they would be up in front of the group. Think from the audience's point of view and do whatever it takes to break up boring material so you don't lose your listeners totally.

Joan Eisenstodt, a former MPI Meeting Planner of the Year says, "High-content, informational speakers almost always fall flat if they don't use some humor. I equate appropriate humor with warmth, and audiences respond to warmth." She also notes, "After 25 years watching audiences and presenters, I know that even subtle humor can help the audience respond positively to information that could be considered boring."

Makes a positive impression. Laughter and good humor create bonds. Even if the audience members don't like you, they will like you better if you can make them laugh or smile and they will leave with better thoughts of you.

Shows that you don't take yourself too seriously. The old saying goes, "If you take yourself too seriously, no one else will." If you can laugh a little bit at yourself at the right times, your audience can laugh with you and not at you.

Helps paint pictures in the audience's mind. The pictures humorous storytellers can paint are what people remember, not the words.

Makes information more memorable. Joyce Saltman, a college professor and well-known speaker in the health care field, did exhaustive research for her 1995 doctoral dissertation "Humor in Adult Learning." She concluded, "Most researchers agreed that humor generally aided in the retention of materials as well as to the enjoyment of the presentation of the information."

Lightens up heavy material. Appropriate humor added to heavy, serious material gives the audience a few seconds to relax. Even Shakespeare employed this device, called "comic relief," extensively to provide distraction or offer respite from the serious events of a tragedy.

Here's my personal experience-based list of what humor can do for you:

You will probably be asked back. If you succeed in your original purpose, you may be asked back. If you also make audience members feel really good by entertaining them at the same time, your chances of being asked back will be much higher.

You will get higher marks on evaluations or more sales. If you make listeners feel good, they will like you better and reflect that in your evaluation scores or increased sales.

You will make more money. If you are a professional presenter, you will be booked more and your fees will rise. If you present as part of your job, then read the next item carefully.

You will be more promotable. Having and conveying a sense of humor is on virtually everyone's list of top leadership skills. A humorous and engaging presentation style will push you up the ladder where good communications skills are a must.

If it's good enough for popes and presidents, it's good enough for you. I don't know about the pope, but I do know that all modern-day presidents are coached extensively on the use of appropriate humor for many of the reasons stated above.

You will make people happy. This is my favorite benefit. I get great satisfaction from knowing that I have brightened someone else's life. I had an executive come up to me after one of my humor seminars and say, "You opened up a whole new world for me." I almost cried right on the spot. I'll never forget it.

Tom Antion is a lively and entertaining keynote speaker and seminar leader. He is an expert in advanced sales presentation technique and modern communication skills. This segment is an excerpt from Tom's book **WAKE 'EM UP Business Presentations** *(Anchor Publishing). Tom can be reached at 800-448-6280.*

The Master Of Ceremonies
by Ty Boyd, CSP, CPAE

This is an area where my expertise rivals just about anyone but Bob Barker or Pat Sajak. Though I have always really enjoyed the emcee role, I never dreamed it would be such a big part of my work. Years of broadcasts, hundreds of pageants, fairs, award ceremonies of every description, the annual International Retailer of the Year Awards in Chicago, the Positive Thinking Rallies, not to mention 18 years at the CPAE Banquet at National Speakers Association, have all sharpened my ax.

What I've learned

There are 12 things I have learned over the years:

1. As emcee, you are the captain of the ship, the host. The members of the audience are your guests. Your job is to make them comfortable, to create a dialogue between them and the various events on the program.

2. The job calls for a sense of theater.

3. You are not the show, but you are responsible for the flow, the housekeeping, often the introductions, and the audience's concerns – the total program.

4. You are not the star, but are still critical to the program's success.

5. This job requires preparation. Do your homework.

6. Either carry survival tools or know where to find them (flashlight, extra script, filler materials, etc.).

7. You are the fire marshal.

8. It's your attitude that shows.

9. Set the stage for real people and a worthy audience. Answer the audience's question of, "What's in it for me?"

10. You are the sergeant-at-arms.

11. Have fun.

12. Don't overstep your boundaries.

You can create a useful talent to enhance your value to the meeting professional. Work hard enough that the meeting planner will want you to return as the emcee next year. Then you can sell a speech to go with it!

The introducer

Too few people are introduced effectively. I always advise speakers to write their own intros. It's sometimes the only commercial you will get. Additionally, I instruct them to print reading instructions on the page with the intro. Simply say, "Please read as written." Funny thing, when we have that instruction on the intro, people will work so much harder to do it well — and just the way you have written it. It beats some clown saying, "Well, here's an old buddy-buddy of mine. Never dreamed we'd be paying him to tell us anything about this subject. Let's give a warm welcome to this fool!"

Being the introducer requires that we create an atmosphere of mutual respect between the audience and the speaker. We need to answer several questions: Why this speaker? At this time? For this audience and at this place? As a speaker you know how much better the event goes when these questions are answered.

Here are some pointers:
- You are the stage-setter.
- Create an inviting environment.
- Do your homework.
- Be really interested in the speaker and subject. Show it.
- Unless the speaker is a celebrity, use his or her name several times. Audiences forget.
- Be a little bit on the gossipy side. Make the introduction sound like a novel, not a textbook. Be sure to answer the audience's unasked question, "What's in it for me?"
- Never introduce a female as "Mrs. John Smith" or

in a sexist way.

- When you make an introduction, speak to the audience, not to the person being introduced.

- Do not upstage or overpraise.

- While you are on stage, you are the captain of the ship. Don't leave the center spot until the speaker has arrived. Welcome the speaker with a handshake, nod, smile or slight touch on the shoulder, then exit. It's now his or her show.

- Model good listening.

- Lead the applause. Model the behavior you would expect from the audience.

You may not be compensated for simply introducing a speaker, but the more proficiency you display on the platform, the more desirable you become as a total package. Many times, the roles of emcee and introducer are combined.

Ty Boyd has been a speaker for 25 years, and is a Cavett Award winner. He founded the Excellence in Speaking Institute in 1980. He can be reached at 800-336-2693.

Voice Training: Who Needs It?

by Ralph E. Hillman, Ph.D.

"My voice is fine, thank-you!" Speakers who say this often experience a variety of voice ailments: sore throats, "tired voices," hoarseness, loss of voice, excessive throat clearing, etc. Speakers attribute these ailments to "fatigue" or "overuse" of their voices. In reality, our voices are not tired or overused, they are abused. How we speak when we are speaking is what hurts us. Most people who have these recurring vocal concerns often exhibit breathy characteristics as well as associated vocal fold tension which results in vocal abuse. Using a breathy voice is OK for emphasis or to soften the glottal attack on initial vowels. Speakers incur vocal ailments when they add excessive vocal tension to an already breathy vocal sound. The exaggerated example would be people shouting at a ballgame. During the second half their voices are gone.

What is breathiness?

During healthy sound production, the vocal folds are pulled together with just enough muscle tension to allow them to be forced apart by air pressure from the diaphragm. These vibrations occur very rapidly; 256 cycles per second for middle C.

In the attempt to make complete closure, additional muscle tension is required, making the vocal folds slam together during each cycle. The unhealthy, habitually breathy voice quality is the result of the vocal folds opening too widely and often not making complete closure with each cycle and thus allowing excessive air to pass between the folds.

You sound different to yourself than the tense voice quality does to others. We hear ourselves primarily as the sound is transmitted from our vocal folds, through bone, cartilage and tissue to our ears. Others hear us with the sound going through the air and then to the ears. Professionals often do not know they are being breathy, because they have not learned to hear it. In addition, breathiness makes the presence of other voice qualities, that is, nasal and muffled, almost impossible to distinguish.

What causes breathiness?

Basically, there are three conditions which prevent the vocal folds from making complete closure and are responsible for the breathy symptoms:

1. The lack of appropriate muscle tension in the vocal folds; these are learned habit patterns which are deeply ingrained in the muscle reflexes themselves. Since speech production is a learned skill, the habit of keeping the muscles of the vocal folds too loose during speech production can be changed. You can voluntarily control that pattern by using a more tense voice quality; cut down on the amount of air exhaled during speech.

2. The lack of sufficient muscle tension around the back of the posterior end of the vocal folds (the oblique and transverse arytenoid muscles, that pull the arytenoid cartilages and the posterior ends of the vocal folds together), resulting in an interarytenoid notch or vocal "chink" at the posterior end of the vocal folds. This is space that allows air to pass between the folds before, during and after speech production, regardless of the muscle tension of the vocal folds. These muscles can be

strengthened with the trill/swallow exercise.

3. The presence of a polyp, nodule, carcinoma or some other pathology which prevents the vocal folds from adducting or coming together; these are often the result of improper functioning of the vocal folds. Consult an ear, nose and throat specialist (sometimes abbreviated ENT or more precisely identified as an otolaryngologist) if you suspect you might have a problem you are not able to change or correct using the suggestions found here.

Where do I begin?

For the first step, let us look at the standard assumptions regarding our general physical health. Since each of them can have an effect on speech production, most people need to heed these before starting voice training. These assumptions will not be detailed here, because they really are self-explanatory. If you do have questions regarding these assumptions, contact me directly.

- Eat right. Avoid milk and other dairy products, chocolate, soft drinks and sugar/sweeteners before speaking, or any foods which you know thicken the saliva in your mouth. Help your voice and body as a whole to stay healthy.

- Drink water, eight glasses a day, to cleanse the body and keep the vocal folds moist.

- Use Entertainers Secret,™ a great nose and throat moisturizer, to lubricate and open up your nose and throat.

- Do weekly aerobic exercise; do a daily routine to keep your heart healthy and your muscles limber.

- Get adequate sleep, maintaining consistent body clock hours (getting up and going to bed at the same time).

- Minimize exposure to dust, smoke and noise.

- Avoid alcohol and recreational drugs, and follow the advice of health care professionals before taking any medications. If you have diabetes, asthma, high blood pressure, clinical depression, etc., you can't avoid drugs. Just be careful to avoid abusing them.

- Keep a positive focus: Maintain a positive attitude and work at smiling, which releases healing endorphins.

Utilizing these suggestions will help make sure your body is healthy and ready for you to speak effectively.

What? I need to work on posture, neck & shoulder muscle tension and my breathing?

The second step calls for mastering the "Big Three." Mastery of these three separate physical areas will not guarantee you "perfect" speech, but most people can hear a difference in the improved sound.

A) Posture or stance

The six essentials for good posture:

- Unlock your knees while standing. OK, you knew that. Locking your knees cuts off the blood flow to your brain. Ever watch people who are standing at attention pass out?

- Keep your pelvis level, not too far forward or back.
- Tuck your tummy, keeping it firm from the belly-button down.
- Raise your rib cage; be able to feel the bottoms of your ribs all the time, not just while speaking.
- Keep your shoulders back and down. It will look and feel military.
- Keep your head up on top. A straight line goes from the top of your ear to the top of your shoulder to the top of your hip to the center of your foot.

A lifetime activity of good posture needs to be checked at least once an hour, for every hour you are awake, for the rest of your life. Make the commitment! Check your posture with your body parallel to a wall. If your head is well forward of the perpendicular line of the wall, or your shoulders are rolled forward, or your rib cage is down, or your pelvis is tipped, the following are likely to be affected or result:

1. the flow of oxygen-rich blood to your brain
2. restricted breathing
3. tongue pulled back, making clear diction difficult
4. elevated pitch-muscles of the larynx are tight and the vocal folds are not free to move
5. arytenoids pulled apart, imposing a breathy sound allowing air to pass even when it's unintended
6. muscles of the larynx affecting tense or relaxed vocal fold closure.

Thus, your posture can affect the breathiness of your vocal production.

Do this exercise: Put your hands (palms forward) up and back against the wall at shoulder height (in the "I give up" position). Placing a "Hillman Handle" (a broom handle) in back of your shoulder blades with the wrists of your hands in back of that handle can help you position the shoulders. Now the "I give up" position can become a reality. Keep your head up on top and elevate your rib cage. If you cannot hold that position for any length of time, your shoulders have been pulled forward for too long. Over time, pulling your shoulders back and straightening your spine down will relax your whole body. Now try counting to five. Contrast that count to five with a count when you are using your old posture. You should sound much louder and clearer when up against the wall. Ultimately, this posture allows the larynx to be free of excessive external muscle tension that might restrict or inhibit efficient vocal fold movement.

If the military bearing of this posture activity may feel stiff and awkward, you are on the right track. You do not need to be rigid, but you do need to sit and stand with erect posture. The erect posture should be your "home" position. Be free to move around, but when you are finished moving, return to the "home" position. Check yourself in the mirror or record yourself on video. Ask friends and family how you and your new posture look to them. Some will complain that you look stiff and vigil. Thank them for noticing. Most of them will prefer the more alert and attentive bearing of your body. Soon your face will reflect the relaxed condition of the rest of your body.

Those who make a consistent attempt to maintain their new posture often begin to experience a self-concept shift. Most people feel more positive about themselves and more in control of who they are – especially on the platform.

B) Relax neck and shoulder muscles

Avoid tension of the muscles on the front and sides of your neck, for any reason. Even though our posture is straightened, and we should be physically relaxed, it is very possible for us to keep our neck and shoulder muscles in a tense condition. Many speakers persist in staying in this condition, because often they are not aware the condition exists, or believe those behaviors indicate emotional interest in the audience they are addressing. Although easily overlooked, detection of tense neck and shoulder muscles is crucial. Besides, tightening the neck muscles and/or thrusting your head forward as a result is ugly. Put your hand to your neck to feel the tension while breathing and speaking, or watch for tension in a mirror or on video. When the neck and shoulder muscles are tight, the muscle movement in and around the larynx is inhibited. This phenomenon directly impacts the sound of your voice.

C) Breath support

Diaphragmatic breathing involves using muscles of the diaphragm which attach at the base of the rib cage and hump up into the chest cavity. When breathing most efficiently, the muscle activity and movement will be around the torso between the bellybutton and base of the sternum. The ribs should move sideways. Keep your tummy firm from the bellybutton down, expanding the rib cage sideways using the upper abdominal muscles without raising your shoulders or puffing out the lower abdominal cavity (our lungs are not down there).

To obtain the most value from diaphragmatic breathing, utilize a "Cleansing Breath," which really can be a valuable stress reduction tool. Dr. Richard Quisling of Summit Medical Center, Donelson, Tenn., calls this a Cleansing Breath because it provides the lungs and your body with the cleansing effect of more oxygen.

Performing a Cleansing Breath is simple: Keeping your posture erect (using the steps to good posture and keeping the head up with shoulders back and down), relax your neck and shoulder muscles completely, which fills the lungs, allowing air to enter through your nose freely and easily. Now, completely empty your lungs BY FORCING THE AIR OUT, by blowing through pursed lips, under pressure using your diaphragm. To know that you are getting the full benefit of a Cleansing Breath, place your hands around the abdominal area at your sides. You should feel this area moving in and out, expanding sideways. Now repeat. A Cleansing Breath will relax your spirit, voice and body. While you are doing the lifetime hourly posture routine, practice doing Cleansing Breaths.

Breathing contrast exercise: Test the impact of the oxygen exchange when doing a Cleansing Breath. Do four Cleansing Breaths in a row with the lip constriction and lots of air pressure from the diaphragm. After you have done the four Cleansing Breaths, note the strong possibility that you are experiencing a head rush. Now, for contrast, using the Big Three, fill your lungs and gently release the air with no constrictions and minimal air pressure. No head rush! By forcing out the air, you are encouraging a greater oxygen exchange in your lungs and getting more oxygen into your blood. That oxygen-rich blood is spread throughout your body, and some of it actually makes its way to your brain. The benefits of additional oxygen in your brain should be obvious. Regular Cleansing Breaths strengthen the diaphragm muscles, providing more breath support for speech.

What can I do to hear breathiness?

The third step is to listen to other people in whom the breathiness is obvious. It is easier to hear breathiness in others first. You also might want to note the values you attach to the personalities of those who habitually use the breathy voice quality. Typical stereotypes of habitually breathy speakers include weak, passive or sexy. As speakers we need to occasionally use the breathy voice quality for emphasis to indicate those qualities as perceived, as well as being soft and gentle or compassionate. Learning more about the stereotypes associated with voice qualities is an interesting study; but that is another article.

To hear breathiness in yourself, do the breathy contrast exercise: Try counting aloud from three to nine, exhaling lots of air as you count. Use the flat of your hand in front of your mouth to feel the amount of air being expelled. The vocal folds are trying to operate efficiently by making complete closure during each cycle, but they are unable to do so because of the lack of appropriate vocal fold tension which would restrict the airflow.

Now, contrast the breathy voice quality with the production of a much more tense sound. In a rather staccato fashion, cutting off the end of the sound of each word, do the count again. You should sound louder and feel less air passing out of your mouth and hitting your hand as you count. Do this negative practice, exaggerating both conditions. Once you are aware of the differences, you may choose to use varying degrees of breathiness anywhere along the continuum.

Standing push-up exercise: With your feet 18 to 24 inches from the wall, your hands on the wall at shoulder level, say "ah" as you let your rigid body lean toward the wall, bending only at your ankles. When your head is a few inches from the wall, stop the forward movement and the "ah" sound. You should hear and feel the vocal folds close. As you approach the wall you should hear the breathiness diminish. Now try to mimic that closure without doing the push-up. Being aware of the sound of breathiness will be enough to diminish its use.

What exercises will help me change my breathy habit?

1. Trill/swallow.

Strengthen the muscles holding the arytenoids together.

a) With good posture, relaxed neck and shoulders, and efficient breath support, initiate a Cleansing Breath (fill your lungs).

b) Elevate your chin toward the ceiling.

c) Trill your tongue off the alveolar ridge (or rapidly tap your tongue off the gum ridge behind your upper front teeth).

d) Hum, going up in pitch.

e) When you hit your highest pitch, swallow (if you can't swallow, lower your chin slightly and try again).

f) Keeping your chin elevated, restart the trill, coming down in pitch to your lowest pitch.

g) Do another Cleansing Breath.

2. Echo. Reduce breathiness by producing an echo off a wall, to make vocal fold movement more efficient. This is not a volume exercise. This exercise can also be done by bouncing the sound off the windshield of a car. If you do not hear an echo, you are probably being too breathy.

If you must persist in being habitually breathy, the least

you can do is avoid glottal attacks. Glottal attacks occur primarily on vowels which are the first voiced sounds of words. The vocal folds are brought together quickly and with excessive pressure to make the sound sharp and clear. You can avoid this vocal abuse by connecting these initial vowel sounds to the last sound of the previous word. So avoid "punching" or stressing words that begin with a vowel.

Even though you may not think you need voice training, EVERY TIME BEFORE YOU SPEAK do a voice warm-up: Be sure the "Big Three" are in place. Hum at optimum pitch (four to eight pitches up from your lowest pitch), and at a soft volume. Resist breathiness. Then hum, expanding the range slowly up and down the scale as you get louder. Take at least five minutes.

Awareness is the key. Take full advantage of this breathiness information by doing the contrast practice, so you can learn to hear it. Listen, as you practice to control it. Remember, there is nothing wrong with being breathy, just do not add the tense voice quality to it. Speakers can use breathiness to their advantage only if they know how to control it.

Ralph E. Hillman, Ph.D., The Speaker Who Speaks With Speakers About Speaking, author of **Communication Strategies, Work For Your Voice,** *and* **Delivering Powerful Presentations: Use Your Voice and Body for Impact** *(published by Allyn & Bacon) is a keynote speaker and speaking coach who teaches at Middle Tennessee State University in Murfreesboro, Tenn.*

Call 615-898-2271, fax 615-898-5826, or e-mail rhillman@frank.mtsu.edu

Six Principles Of Audience-Centered Seating™

by Paul O. Radde, Ph.D.

Proper room arrangements can affect the interaction of the group and its response to the speaker. This is something most speakers and meeting planners rarely consider.

Here are six basic principles for planning and trouble-shooting any presentation setup:

1. Set the room toward the long wall so that participants can be closer to the presenter and facilitators. This makes the exchange more inclusive and personal. Those in front can be more intimate. Those in the back are still closer than they would be in a "bowling alley" setup facing the narrow wall.

2. Curve the seating – no straight rows. Curved rows promote learning, comfort, safety, networking, bonding, line of sight and capacity. If you will entertain a group discussion or problem-solving session, place the group in a semi-circle facing visual surfaces such as a screen or flip charts. Then you can occupy the open area in the middle and step in front of attacks of one member or another, and redirect group attention and energy back to the agenda item, problem or issue at hand.

3. Flare the aisles out 45 degrees from the platform

edge toward the exits – no center aisle. Center aisles tend to drain energy from the presentation, and eliminate the best seats in the house. Flared aisles provide greater carrying capacity and traffic on aisles near the doors where volume is greatest.

4. Face each chair directly toward the presentation. The most symmetrical room setup may appear to be neat and orderly, but it may wreak havoc on the spines of those seated. Facing each chair may not be as neat, but it provides maximum comfort and line of sight for the participant.

5. Cut single-chair-width access lanes into the larger seating sections. This ensures ease of access to chairs. Latecomers tend to stand in the back rather than cross over in front of several seated participants to get to a middle seat. Access lanes increase the number of easy access seats, and aid traffic flow, getting participants in and out faster during breaks to keep the meeting on schedule.

6. In crowded, smaller meeting rooms, set the back row along the back wall. Leave an aisle in front of the back row which is more likely to stay unimpeded in the event of an emergency exit. If the room is really crowded, and cannot accommodate everyone seated, then leave the back of the room open for a greater number to stand.

While not directly related to seating arrangements, don't forget to light the faces of those who will address the group. Many audience members have impaired hearing and read lips to fully understand. They may not even be aware of this fact. However, if they can't see you, they can't hear you. And the misunderstanding or failure to keep up with exchanges can muddle the meeting. Lighting the face of the speaker is really essential, but curiously enough, is not being done in many instances.

Paul O. Radde, Ph.D., provides keynotes and seminars on Thriving: Taking Your Life to the Next Level, and runs the Audience Centered Seating Institute™. He can be reached at 800-966-8333.

Power, Punch And Pizzazz

by Ray Pelletier

Whoever you are...whatever your particular style...whatever the subject...whatever the makeup of your audience ... there are several fundamentals to keep in mind when designing a motivational presentation.

The first and foremost is to develop a solid mind-set that you are there to meet the needs of your audience. This is more than just something you tell yourself; it has to be YOUR motivation for being there in the first place. And it has to show – it has to be perfectly obvious to everyone in the room. The old axiom is a fact: Nobody cares how much you know until they know how much you care. Unless you are motivated by that great truth, and believe and practice it thoroughly, I suggest you change your line of work; you're unlikely to serve your client properly or to motivate any audience. With the audience's needs in mind, pre-program research becomes essential. The client can give you a summation of the problems that need to be solved, but it is up to you to conduct your own research into the audience attitudes and feelings you'll be encountering. This is the only way you'll know how to relate to your listeners and reach them on a personal level where you can accomplish what the client has asked of you. As professional speaker Phil Wexler put it, "Prescription without diagnosis is malpractice."

I've carried out pre-program research in a number of ways. One way is through questionnaires to prospective audience members (the list being supplied by the meeting planner). I assure confidentiality and ask recipients of the questionnaire for their views about such subjects as competition, product quality/service, marketing, teamwork, corporate communication and their general feelings about the company and their jobs and whatever problems they may be having. It's amazing what you can learn about the corporate culture from such a questionnaire – it can sometimes be very different from the snapshot you get from a meeting planner.

But by far the most productive research method is to arrange for casual, one-on-one interviews with several prospective members of the audience at some point before the seminar. Face-to-face meetings enable you to sense nuances that won't be obvious in the written answers to a questionnaire. An added benefit of personal interviews is that you'll be able to look out at your audience during a seminar and see people you've met and whose attitudes and feelings you know. You'll better understand how to reach them. And if your several interviewees are reasonably representative of the audience as a whole (almost invariably the case), you'll have found the hot buttons that can reach and motivate most, if not all, of your listeners. They'll have no doubt that you're speaking to THEM, with THEIR needs in mind. They'll be surprised. They'll find it refreshing. They'll respect you. And they will listen.

The meeting ENVIRONMENT is another matter you should attend to with great care. That it should be friendly, welcoming and positive goes without saying. But it is also extremely important that the meeting room, and the way it is set up, reflects your message in an exciting and entertaining way. In my case, it isn't unusual to see signage all over the walls as well as bullet-point placards that will reinforce my message as I go along. Props, such as ladders, chairs, luggage and other odd items that will be used to animate and illustrate segments of my message are often in full view on- and offstage. People see all this as they come into the room. They wonder about it. They're curious. There's an excitement about it. It puts them in an expectant mood. They're here for a real show. It's fun.

Well-chosen props are learning and remembrance aids that invariably drive home a point far more dramatically than words alone. If it's not your habit to use them, I suggest you experiment a little bit. Just try it. Even the most serious and somber seminar can benefit from a choice prop or two. Props bring words to life. And I often include music and video clips in that mix.

Audience involvement and participation is another of the fundamental points motivational speakers will be wise to keep in mind. The more audience members are involved in a presentation, the more they'll enjoy and remember it.

SPEAKING STYLE, of course, is a matter of individual taste and purpose, and I won't presume to suggest one. But here, again, a common advantage is available to any speaker who can sprinkle selected anecdotes and parables throughout his or her message. This is a tried, true and much-honored method of adding flavor and understanding to any subject – from the most lighthearted anecdote to the most serious and profound story.

Simplicity and clarity are also common fundamentals ... the real "master keys" to effective communicating. Before I walk onto a platform, I invariably remind myself of this: KISS - Keep It Simple, Simon! This is not a sign of disrespect toward an audience. It is a sign of the very highest respect. I have no intention of confusing an audience and wasting the time of a few hundred people who are just as bright, perceptive and smart as I am. They deserve a non-ambiguous message that can be understood immediately. Crafting that kind of message – going over it again and again with an eye to absolute clarity – is an essential discipline, no matter what your speaking style may be.

Sometimes, in my seminars, I ask everybody to start conversing with the people beside them in language geared to 8-year-olds. No big words. Just childhood language.

They love it! The energy is really high in the room. But, most importantly, audience members learn that when they speak as simply as possible there is never any confusion about what is being said. Everyone understands everyone else.

Here they are, all grown-up and sophisticated — and yet the best way to be sure they're understood by everyone at all times is to speak in the simple, non-ambiguous language of childhood!

The real bottom line to successful motivational speaking can probably be summed up this way: The privilege of the platform is to be taken literally. It is a privilege — and a great responsibility — to mold and motivate an audience. If you consistently bear that in mind, you can't help but be audience-oriented and you will instinctively come to understand the basics that are necessary to success — the fundamentals that are necessary for you to put on a memorable program with power, punch and pizzazz.

It all comes down to being there for THEM, not for yourself. All audience members in the world know the difference – and, I promise you, they will respond accordingly. *Ray Pelletier – known as "America's Business Attitude Coach"– is an international keynoter, seminar leader and management consultant. Expansion on the material in this article can be found in his new, best-selling book,* **Permission to Win** *(Oakhill Press). Ray can be reached at 1-800-SPEAKER.*

Selling As A Life Skill

by Tim Connor, CSP

Many people only look at selling as selling products or services. In this section we will look at the concept of selling as the ability to influence and persuade people. Everyone sells or doesn't sell every day. Parents sell values, morals and ethics, teachers sell study habits and learning as a lifelong process, politicians sell their ideas or platforms, managers sell policies and procedures and children sell 24 hours a day for the better part of their early lives. They do not sell a product or service, or have ever attended a sales seminar or read a book on sales, but can they ever sell. I will bet wherever you live, there are several hundred people who will apply for new positions today. Most will have the experience, talent and qualifications but will not be selected because they lack the ability to sell themselves.

Getting a good seat in a restaurant, asking your boss for a raise, and everything else in life requires this vital ability. You either get what you want in life or you don't. Most of the people who don't, lack the ability to influence and persuade others.

Let's discuss the attitude concepts, behaviors and skills that people who get what they want effectively use.

Attitude concepts

There are several concepts that impact your ability to successfully influence and persuade people. The most important ones are self-image, self-confidence, self-worth, your goals and your ability to effectively communicate.

Self-image is how you feel about yourself. If you don't like yourself, it will be difficult to convince others that you deserve what it is you are trying to sell or get. Self-confidence is having the attitude that you can successfully handle whatever comes your way regardless of obstacles, difficulty or circumstances. You trust yourself. Self-worth is when you value what you know, can do and believe in, regardless of the opinions, actions or feelings of others. Your goals are the direction in life you are traveling. Clear goals contribute to your ability to see into the future with hope, vision, passion and purpose. Your ability to communicate effectively is a function of your vocabulary, desire to express your thoughts clearly, your willingness to listen and understand, and the courage to say what you mean and mean what you say.

These attitude concepts dramatically influence your ability to effectively persuade others. Without them, it will be difficult to achieve any real power. (I am using power as your ability to have congruence between your values, beliefs, thoughts and actions).

Behaviors

Behavior is how you act out daily – your purpose and goals, or lack of them, your inner feeling and attitudes, and your beliefs and values. Personality is one way we define ourselves to the surrounding world. Are you sending a clear message that you know what you want, have the ability to get it and will pursue it until you are successful, or are you sending the message that you are a victim and not worthy of other people's attention, time, energy and interest?

Ever notice how some people achieve greater life success than others? Want to know the common denominator in every case where this is true? I have been discussing it for several minutes. It is their ability to influence and persuade others; to sell themselves, their ideas, their products, their needs and desires.

Skills

Now that we have briefly set the stage, let's discuss a few practical tips that can improve your ability in this critical area of life. We'll break these skills into five major areas:

a) the ability to get information

b) the ability to see clearly (to manage your perceptions)

c) the ability to give information that is consistent with your intent

d) the ability to ensure that the other party or parties have understood your meaning and intent

e) the ability to have a clear awareness of your objectives.

The ability to get information

The person that asks the questions controls the conversation, the person who talks the most dominates it. The key to gaining influence is not what you say but what you know. The use of information is power. Questions are the best way to get information. There are two major types of questions: open and closed. Open questions ask for feelings, attitudes, opinions and general information. Closed questions ask for a yes or no or a specific fact. Closed questions shut down further dialogue and open questions encourage more response. The key to getting information, so that you can decide what information is useful to use, is to ask more open than closed questions.

The ability to see clearly

Life is a perceptual experience. No one looks at life and its circumstances the same. This gives life its color, uniqueness and diversity as well as a great deal of frustration, conflict and misunderstanding. To see life from another person's perspective requires a lot of insight, flexibility, ego control, compassion and emotional maturity.

To see life as it really is requires that you remain open to change, receptive to other points of view and that you let go of old emotional baggage and attachments. It also requires that you let go of future attachments to outcomes of certain events and people. Neither of these are easy to accomplish but are necessary to see life as it really is, not as you would like it to be.

The ability to give information

The tools we use to send information are verbal and non-verbal messages. Verbal messages represent a small portion of the overall communication message. If there is an inconsistency between the words and the non-verbal signals you send, you will confuse the other person. Also, if you are receiving mixed signals, both verbal and non-verbal, the non-verbal will always be more accurate. This is primarily true because non-verbal signals come from a person's unconscious mind and are not within his or her conscious control. Yes, we can send dedicated, conscious non-verbal signals when we are trying to send a particular message to another person but these happen less than the natural unconscious signals.

The verbal method of sending information is with words. The purpose of a good vocabulary is to give you flexibility with your choice of words. A good vocabulary is one of the most important skills to develop to improve your ability to influence and persuade. Without a good vocabulary you will find yourself limited in your use of appropriate or persuasive language. However, remember that the purpose of communication is to express yourself, not impress people. Don't use big words if a smaller one will get the job done.

The ability to ensure understanding

I will guarantee that in the past 48 hours you have had a misunderstanding with someone. I will bet it was do to one of the following causes: assumptions were made, expectations were not communicated, the pace of the delivery was faster or slower than you are comfortable with, there were hidden agendas or it was poor listening habits by you or the other party or parties.

The ability to have a clear awareness of your objectives

If a ship doesn't reach the harbor, it isn't the harbor's fault. To get what you want, you have to know what you want. This, at first glance, might seem to be a simplistic cliché. However, after more than 30 years in sales and 20 years teaching selling, it is my conclusion that most people just wing their way through life, hoping that what they want will magically come to them without any clear objectives, plan or action.

A general goal will tend to give you general behavior, therefore general results. Specific goals will give you specific behavior and give you more specific results.

Let's wrap it up

To successfully sell, influence and persuade people, it is necessary to communicate with clarity and focus, have confidence in your beliefs, values and life philosophy and know your objectives. And it is vital that you live with congruence and passion.

It is also critical that you understand that the principles used by today's top salespeople to sell their products and services are no different than the skills necessary to get your dream job or influence a group of people in a professional presentation.

Tim Connor, CSP, has been a full-time speaker and sales and management trainer since 1974. He is the author of the international best seller, **Soft Sell** *(Source Books), now in its 29th printing, and* **Sales Mastery, Secrets of Six-Figure-Income Salespeople** *(Connor Resource Group). Each issue of his popular newsletter Life Balance is read by more than 7,500 people. You can reach him at 800-222-9070, or visit him on the Internet: http://www.TimConnor.com*

Presentation Skills For Trainers

by Karen Lawson, Ph.D., CSP

Like it or not, today's trainers are also performers. It's becoming increasingly more difficult to gain and maintain program participants' attention and interest. Today's corporate classroom audiences expect and demand to be entertained as well as trained. They want the learning experience to be both meaningful and enjoyable. Although challenging, meeting these needs and expectations is not difficult if you incorporate interactive techniques in your training design.

Get them active from the start

Participant involvement is critical to the success of your training program. "People learn by doing, not by being told," a basic principle of adult learning, should be your guide in designing any training program, from the highly technical to the so-called "soft skills" addressed in human resource development programs.

From the very beginning, participants need to be engaged. You can create immediate involvement with a variety of fun, yet content-related activities and techniques. Opening activities can accomplish several goals:

1. involving the participants immediately in the learning experience
2. creating a risk-free learning environment
3. communicating personal responsibility for learning
4. introducing the content
5. building group cohesiveness
6. assessing participant needs and expectations

Be sure to choose an opening activity that will accomplish several goals or objectives. For example, one very successful technique is called, "What Do You Want to Know?" You, the trainer, post flip chart pages on the wall, each with a heading that corresponds to the major topics of the training program. Then give a packet of Post-it™ notes to each participant and ask the participants to write down questions they have about any of the topics. They may fill as many notes as desired, but put only one question per note. The participants then get up and place their questions under the appropriate headings. You can then categorize the questions and compare them to the learning objectives of the session. This method gives participants an opportunity to express their expectations anonymously. They are also immediately engaged in the process, thinking about the content, and beginning to take ownership for their learning. The only goal this activity does not meet is building group cohesiveness.

Involving your audience

Group involvement, a critical component of an effective training session, is easy if you follow the principles and practices of cooperative or peer learning. Cooperative learning is the instructional use of small groups so that participants work together to maximize their own and each other's learning. For our purpose, a small group can be as few as two people or as many as eight. As trainers, we need to keep two very important principles in mind:

1. learning by nature is an active endeavor
2. different people learn in different ways

With those principles in mind, trainers need to use a variety of methods that will ensure a high level of participation and a moderate level of content.

The trainer needs to create many opportunities for the participants to interact with each other. Often this may involve asking people to work in pairs to come up with a joint answer to a question posed by the trainer, prepare a list of guidelines related to the topic, or discuss individual responses. Pairs ensure 100 percent participant involvement in a low-risk environment.

The use of small groups is a very effective way to get

people involved. Use small groups to generate ideas, discuss concepts, solve problems or work on case studies. Small groups provide more opportunities for people to contribute and participate. Often those who are reluctant to speak up in a large group situation seem to "come alive" when placed in a small group setting.

Interacting with the audience

Many trainers use role-playing as a skill-building technique in their training programs. More often than not, this technique does not achieve the desired results because of participant resistance. One very effective, non-threatening way of using role-playing is to conduct a demonstration role-play. You would have prepared a scripted role-play depicting either the right way or wrong way of using a particular skill, technique or process. Early in the session, select two "actors" from the group and give them the script so they will have an opportunity to familiarize themselves with their parts prior to the demonstration. At the appropriate point in the program, ask the "players" to come forward and simply read their scripts while the rest of the group observes the interaction for various do's and don'ts that illustrate the learning points.

Another non-threatening role-playing technique involves the trainer as one of the role-players. Ask for a volunteer to come up front and assume the role of the other person. For example, in a "Customer Service" session, you want to demonstrate how to deal with an irate customer.

You assume the role of the customer service representative and ask for a volunteer to play the irate customer who is returning a piece of merchandise for a full refund. The "employee" (played by the trainer) is not permitted to give a refund, only store credit. As the role-playing begins, the "customer" demands a refund. At this point, you stop the action and turn to the participants for coaching. When the action resumes, you as the employee follow the group's suggestions in responding to the customer. This stop-action technique is used several times throughout the role-playing.

Trainers who want to promote interaction will often use open-ended questions to encourage participation. Although this technique is useful, its biggest flaw is that generally a handful of people respond. Many trainers complain that the same people are answering all the questions or offering input. There are several techniques that will guarantee 100 percent audience response. One method is to use response cards. Hand each participant cards to use in responding to multiple choice (A,B,C,D) or true-false (T,F) questions. Develop three or four statements or questions to which participants will respond with their cards. As you read (or show) each item, participants will respond by holding up the card of their choice.

Another way to get every person to respond is to use an active response system. Choose four or five questions or statements designed to get participants to express their opinions about a certain topic. For example, to introduce the topic of "Managing Conflict" you might choose the following statements:

- Conflict is inevitable.
- Conflict increases during times of change.
- Conflict can lead to either creative or dysfunctional results.
- Conflict should be encouraged.

You would ask participants to stand. As you display the first statement, ask participants to remain standing if they agree with the statement and sit down if they disagree. Then ask a few people to explain why they agreed or disagreed before moving to the next statement. An alternative approach would be to ask participants to hold up cards with an "A" for agree and "D" for disagree.

Using theatrical techniques

It's show time! Each training session should be a carefully crafted and choreographed production enhanced and enlivened by the use of theatrical techniques, including props, costumes and staging. The idea is to make the training experience memorable.

A great way to start is to have a theme. For example, for a team-building session, you might choose a sports theme. Training materials would include sports graphics such as pictures of people playing sports and various sports equipment. To reinforce your message of the importance of creating a team environment, bring props to the session. Use a referee's whistle to bring the group back together at the end of a group activity. Use baseball caps to indicate team leaders. When you break into subgroup activities, you could group people by different sports. For example, one group might be baseballs; another basketballs; and others could be footballs, soccer balls, tennis racquets, hockey sticks, etc. Pictures of these various pieces of sports equipment would indicate the location of each subgroup in the room or breakout rooms. Or if you choose to use one sport as a central theme – let's say football – then each subgroup would be assigned the name of a professional football team. You could play recorded team "fight songs" to create the mood as participants enter the room or during breaks. To encourage participation, reward participants with "prizes" of sports paraphernalia such as miniature sports balls, key chains, etc. You could also use sports items attached to cards listing key learning points as giveaways. These little reminders are powerful reinforcement tools. If you're really adventurous, you might even come to the session dressed as a referee, a football player or cheerleader. One thing's for sure – you'll get their attention!

If your comfort zone calls for the less dramatic, you can still use props as metaphors to make your point and reinforce the learning. For example, in a session on change, you might show a Slinky™ to illustrate the need for flexibility. The "Magic Eye" posters are a great way to show how we need to look beyond the obvious and see things differently. A compass can be used in a session on goal-setting to represent the need for direction. The possibilities are endless, and you are bound only by your imagination.

Creating word pictures

Powerful presentation skills include the ability to create mental images, whether you're on the stage or in the classroom. Mental imagery or visualization can be very effective in helping participants create a picture in their minds and overcome obstacles. For example, in a "Presentation Skills" class, the trainer might use visualization to help participants overcome stage fright. You would start by playing relaxation music to create the mood. You would then ask participants to close their eyes, relax and begin breathing deeply. Next, ask them to picture a favorite place where they feel safe, relaxed and comfortable. Give them a few minutes to create that picture in their minds. Next, ask them to picture themselves in front of an audience and then ask the following questions:

- What are you wearing?
- What time of day is it?
- What does the room look like?
- What kind of lighting do you have?
- How many people are there?
- What are you talking about?

Next ask them to visualize themselves at the end of their presentation. They have just delivered a flawless speech. The audience is smiling, standing and clapping with enthusiasm. Give the participants a little time to "savor the moment." After they have had an opportunity to "experience" their taste of success, ask them to open their eyes and discuss with the person next to them how they felt. Most people will respond that they felt very good and enjoyed the feeling of success. The message here, of course, is for them to use this technique to help overcome stage fright every time they are asked to make a presentation or give a speech.

Another powerful technique trainers can use to reinforce their learning points is to tell stories – stories from their own experiences. Stories help the trainer relate to the group, and they help the participants identify with the trainer. Not only does storytelling help create a high trust level between trainer and participants, stories help the message come alive. For example, in a "Presentation Skills" class, I have shared my story about going blank and completely forgetting my speech during a speech contest in high school. I tell the story to illustrate the danger of memorizing and over-preparing. The story also illustrates the point that although it was an embarrassing and traumatic experience, I didn't let it stop me. Here I am many years later – a professional speaker!

Bringing it to a close

Endings are just as important as the rest of the training program. Remember: It's not what you give them, but what they take away that counts. There are many activities you can use to make your training unforgettable. Remember the "What Do You Want to Know" activity where participants wrote their questions and expectations on Post-it™ notes? To bring your training session full circle, ask the participants to get up and reclaim or take off their notes if their question or expectation was addressed. If you've done your job, then the flip chart pages on the wall will be empty. Not only does this activity bring closure to the session, it reinforces the learning. By reclaiming their questions, the participants have taken ownership and are acknowledging that their needs have been met.

Another effective closing technique is the human continuum. At the end of a training session, post two signs, one at each end of a long wall. For example, one sign might read "Competent" and the other, "Clueless." Ask the participants to envision the wall as a continuum. Ask them to think about where they were in terms of their knowledge of the subject and/or skill level at the beginning of the session. Then ask them to stand up and place themselves where they think they were on the continuum. Then ask a few participants to share why they placed themselves where they did. Next ask them to think about where they are on the continuum at the end of the program and place themselves accordingly. Once again, ask participants to share the reasons for their placement. Most people will have moved from the "Clueless" end to the "Competent." Sometimes, however, the reverse happens. Those who come to the session thinking they "know it all" will often discover that they didn't know as much as they thought they did. Consequently, they will indicate a movement in the opposite direction. In either case, this activity is a powerful way to help participants assess how much they perceive they have learned.

Like any other presentation, a successful training session is the result of careful planning, preparation and practice. Effective trainers use a skillful blend of content and participant interaction to create a program that not only involves and informs but influences others to assimilate new information, modify attitudes and change behaviors in both their professional and personal lives.

*Karen Lawson, Ph.D., CSP, international speaker, writer and consultant, is president of Lawson Consulting Group in Lansdale, PA. She is the author or co-author of six books, including **The Art of Influencing** (Kendall/Hunt Publishing Company), and has published dozens of articles in professional journals. You can reach her at 800-269-0797.*

Touching Your Audience's Minds & Hearts With Stories

by Joanna Slan

In an age where people expect to be entertained, and click a button to change channels if they aren't, great speakers must be great storytellers or risk losing their audiences. Whether you are talking about attitude, team building or total quality, spellbinding stories help you grab and hold people's attention.

Listen to people at any get-together, and you will hear stories. We think in stories, and we talk in stories, and our lives form dynamic stories as each day unfolds. The stories told by professional speakers are no different than the stories you tell your friends over a cup of coffee, with one exception: Professional speakers find, tell and remember stories deliberately, not haphazardly.

Professional speakers use stories for a variety of reasons:

1. Stories illustrate major points. The best speakers support main points by inviting listeners to "step into" stories. In becoming the protagonist, the listener is transformed. Because we suffer no consequences by hearing stories, we can savor each moment and still take away valuable lessons. When the topic is controversial, a story may gently explore the more sensitive aspects of a situation. When the point is obscure, a story may hammer home the salient ideas.

2. Stories help us remember new ideas and information. A favorite history teacher of mine in high school made dead people come alive by telling us stories about American pioneers. People remember stories more than isolated information, because stories give information context. This allows the storyteller to share content in an engaging manner.

Recently, a speaker friend of mine received a phone call from a meeting planner. "We're having this conference, and I simply had to call you," explained the meeting planner. "Jane Doe told me the story you told about the secretary who was having a problem. Gee, we all need to hear that story! It was so inspirational. Please send me the information we need to book you."

Long after the speech was over, the story had a life of its own. In chemistry, they teach us that atoms have lives and half-lives, a quantifiable period it takes for the particle to die. Stories seem to take an opposite path. They live on and on, sometimes actually picking up energy and momentum. This helps explain why a book or movie goes from being a "sleeper" to a blockbuster.

3. Stories keep the audience engaged. In school, no matter how boring the teacher, you were forced to sit and listen. In real life, people get up and walk out. If you are lucky, they don't throw vegetables as they walk by.

People hire speakers for their stories. Good speakers work for years to craft messages so compelling that audiences lose all track of time. The finest speakers evoke laughter and tears from their listeners, helping the group to share in a sort of emotional catharsis.

Without using stories, it is difficult, if not impossible to keep the audience interested in what you have to say. Stories keep your audiences entertained and hungry for more.

Human drama

Human drama lies at the heart of all great stories. Classically, there are only three types of human drama: man against man, man against society, and man against God/nature. The movie "The Fugitive" is about man against society, because the protagonist is being tracked down by law enforcement officials (society). "Jaws" is a movie about man vs. nature, with nature taking the form of a shark. "The First Wives Club" is a film about man against man, or to be more accurate, women vs. men.

At its core, human drama parallels the struggles – small and large – that each of us meet on a daily basis. We are not human beings struggling to be spiritual, but rather spiritual beings struggling to be human. In that struggle, we stumble, we fall and we get back up again. Because the struggle is the drama, all stories include some element of change which we also call action.

Too often, speakers connect human drama with human tragedy and ignore the great, but less painful, everyday stories which tell us so much about the nature of being human. A flat tire, missing an airline flight, the hug of a child are at once compelling, human and ubiquitous. Thus, the small triumphs and tribulations of life should not be overlooked, since they represent the fabric of everyday life which we can all understand.

Looking at stories from this view of ordinary life, we see that arguing with a co-worker qualifies as a man-against-man conflict, hitting a deer with the family car exemplifies man against nature, and sitting in a traffic jam serves to prove modern man's daily struggles against society.

Don't miss the best stories you can tell by waiting for high comedy or tragedy. Focus instead on the small drop of water that represents the vast ocean of life.

Where to find good stories

The sages say, "That which is most personal is most universal." By sharing a slice of your life, you connect with your audience in powerful ways. Human beings hunger to know each other. We wonder, "Does anyone understand how I feel?" When we hear stories, we are reassured that the other person is not so different from us. This modern life, filled with alienation and isolation, seems infinitely more bearable when we are not alone.

Where can you find slice-of-life vignettes?

1. What do you tell your spouse, your children or your friends about your day?
2. What was it like for you when you were growing up?
3. What did you overhear while waiting for the bus, train or airplane?
4. What did you see while buying groceries, picking up your child from school, or walking to the mailbox?
5. What made you laugh, cry, smile or get angry as you moved through your day?

You can also find stories by reviewing your entire life. In the movie, "Defending Your Life," Albert Brooks' character dies and goes to a review station before he is sent to either heaven or eternal damnation. By conducting your own life review, you can revive stories that you can use from the platform.

Start by creating a time line. It might look like this:

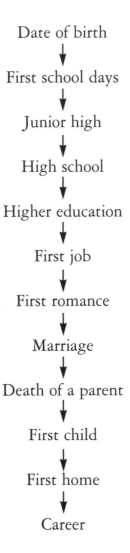

Date of birth
↓
First school days
↓
Junior high
↓
High school
↓
Higher education
↓
First job
↓
First romance
↓
Marriage
↓
Death of a parent
↓
First child
↓
First home
↓
Career

At each juncture, try to fill in a date and a story or two.

Memory-jogging questions:

   1. What is my earliest memory? What was my favorite toy?

2. Which teachers do I remember from grade school? Who was my favorite?

3. What was it like to move on to junior high? Was I scared?

4. What interesting, significant events occurred to me while I was in high school?

5. How did I choose a college? What was my roommate like?

6. When did I get my first job? What did it teach me? What was it?

7. Do I remember my first kiss? Who was it with? What was the setting?

8. What do I remember about my wedding? What was perfect? What went wrong?

9. Have I lost any parents or grandparents? How? What do I miss about that person?

10. What was it like to become a parent? What can I say about my children?

11. Do I remember my first adult home? The first house I bought? The house I brought my first child home to?

12. When did I discover the difference between a job and a career? What are my career high points and low points?

To assist you in your recollections, you may wish to use movies as memory-joggers. If you want to remember high school, watch "American Graffiti" and "Peggy Sue Got Married." To recall the transition from high school to college, check out "The Four Friends" or "Breaking Away." To celebrate your wedding again, view "Four

Weddings and a Funeral" or "Crossing Delancey." To relive the pain of losing an older relative, watch "On Golden Pond." Movies that celebrate the joy of parenthood include "She's Having a Baby" and "Parenthood." To re-connect with the value of having a career, you won't want to miss "Mr. Holland's Opus."

Each movie is not just one story, but a variety of stories woven together. Your life is a rich repository of stories, yours and those of each of your family members. Now might be the perfect time to capture your family memories before you lose someone dear to you and all the wonderful stories that only that person can tell.

Structure of stories

All stories have a beginning, a middle and an end. When we chat with a friend, we may muddy the three, crossing back and forth by saying, "Oh, and I forgot to tell you ... " When you polish your story, systematically arrange the information to produce the biggest bang for your buck.

Start by dividing your story into its three parts. What is the beginning? The listener must have immediate information to locate your story in time and space. Give the listener the essential basics as quickly and concretely as possible: who, what, when, where, how and why.

Now move to the middle. What action or actions propel your story along? Without action, nothing changes.

Change must occur or you don't have a story. Years ago, people amused themselves by creating dramatic tableaus. They would create costumes and scenes which they would then unveil before a home audience to amuse the crowd. Today, we are hooked on action. This modern drug compels us to live restless lives seeking our next hit. Action can be internal, as we think through a problem and develop possible solutions. Or action can be external, as we move and the story moves with us.

Last of all, consider your ending. What is the climax? How is the situation resolved?

Significant detail

As master speaker and storyteller Lou Heckler admonishes speakers, "Don't be the camera. Instead, rob the bank." By skillful use of significant detail, you invite the listener to step into the story rather than to sit passively on the sidelines.

Any concrete, sensory experience offers significant detail. Revisit your story. Ask yourself these questions:

1. What did the situation look like? What were the people involved wearing? Did they have any nervous habits? For example, you could say, "The office was a mess," or you could say, "The office looked like a copier exploded papers all over it." Which is more vivid? The first sentence asks you to believe me. The second paints a picture in your mind.

2. What did the story smell like? In the movie "Michael," the angel smells like baked cookies, reinforcing the idea of life's fleeting homespun joy.

3. What did the story sound like? Humorist Steve Rizzo tells a fabulous story about an acting job he had doing voice-over work for a movie that was to be shown on television. Rizzo was to imitate Jack Nicholson, creating "clean" words and phrases so that the "blue" language in the movie could be replaced. As Rizzo walked around imitating Nicholson, his young son picked up the voice and the attitude. The result was a hilarious encounter with a waitress as young Rizzo looked quizzically at an oversized dessert spoon, and said a la Nicholson, "Gee, lady, did ya hafta bring me a darn shovel?"

4. What did the story taste like? Was there food involved? In every mystery featuring detective V. I. Warsharski, V. I. cooks Italian food for herself when she wants to be comforted. Author Sara Paretsky outlines the ingredients so precisely you could use the novel as a cookbook.

5. What did it feel like? In *At Paradise Gate,* Jane Smiley describes an interaction between mother and child: "Although Anna loved Claire's, and each child's, smiles and waves and kisses, she loved too the stroke of a little hand on her breast while the child nursed, chancing upon this quiet business with a piece of cloth had touched her the most. It was so mysteriously inward

when you hardly yet believed that the child had an inner life." Smiley's writing, so sensual and specific, evokes instant recall to any woman who has ever nursed a child. The author captures two levels of feelings, the kinesthetic and the emotional.

Summary

By finding the stories inherent in your daily life; distinguishing their beginnings, middles and ends; and telling them in such a way to invite your listener to experience them, you will become a spellbinding storyteller.

As with any skill, storytelling grows with practice. Choose a few key stories and work with them. Then try them on everyone you meet. Don't give up easily. Work with the stories, or with a coach, and polish them to perfection.

If we could leave this world but one gift, a gift that touches hearts and unlocks closed minds would assure us that our lives were worthwhile. You can leave that gift by working on your skills as a master storyteller.

Joanna Slan used to tell stories to her little sister Jane when they couldn't sleep. Today, Slan tells stories to keep her audiences awake. Slan is the author of **Storytelling and Humor in Professional Speaking: Opening Minds and Touching Hearts** *(Allyn & Bacon). As a speaker, Slan works with businesses, associations and government agencies to improve their productivity. She can be reached by calling 800-356-2220.*

Presentation Technology: A Picture Speaks A Thousand Words

by Sharon L. Adcock

When planning a presentation, always remember Missouri – the "Show Me" state. Studies indicate that the day after a presentation, the audience can recall only one of 10 key points. However, when a simple graphic is added to the presentation, the audience remembers five key points. Of course, presentation devices and graphics need hardly be simple anymore. There now is a dizzying array of technology that can create sharp, interactive images for use on anything from overheads to VCRs to, yes, the good-old flip chart. Here are some of them:

Photo CD

Eastman Kodak Co. pioneered the technology that allows images from 35mm slides or color negatives to be stored on a compact disc and then viewed on a TV screen. Kodak's standard disc can store 100 images, which can be programmed to appear in a certain order for presentations. The images can be cropped on a computer screen, rotated or zoomed in on for close-ups.

Overheads

Long a staple of presenters, overhead projectors saw a rebirth a few years ago with the development of liquid crystal display (LCD) technology. An LCD panel is placed on an overhead projector and connected to the computer through an interface cable. This allows images from the computer to be projected directly on screen, including text, graphics, scanned images and even full-motion animation. This technology is very popular with speakers who are using laptop computers. One advantage of this development: Images can be created only minutes before a presentation.

Slide projectors

Projectors now have a built-in microprocessor. The projector's stepper motors respond to digital signals from the microprocessor, allowing for the precision needed for multimedia presentations.

Flip charts

Don't scoff, microchip lovers. After all, when Ross Perot wanted to make a point on national TV in his 30-minute infomercials, he turned to flip charts. Of course he didn't win the presidential election even with flip charts, but that's a different story. A portable easel can be folded up and fits into a gun-case-sized pouch that can be slung over the shoulder. And there is now software available that will let you create computer-generated flip charts, which look more professional than handwritten ones.

Video walls

OK, you're not going to cart a video wall to a presentation. But video walls are turning up more and more in large corporate meetings, trade shows and conventions. This once space-age technology promises to become commonplace for larger-size meetings.

Multimedia

The hot buzzword in the computer community and among presenters, multimedia is a combination of different elements such as sound effects, music, computer-generated animation and prerecorded or even live video clips.

Companies that market presentation software practically guarantee their programs will help you mesmerize your audiences. Every presentation, it seems, will be a magical encounter between presenter and audience; the ultimate open-sesame to boundless sales and brilliantly trained personnel. Certainly, software offers remarkable capabilities, but achieving a powerhouse presentation requires adding a few easy-to-learn design principles – and heeding a few cautions. These principles are the same regardless of what computer or software you use, and with minor modifications apply equally well to slides, overheads or electronic media. So, which do you choose?

The number of people, type of room and facilities, time and budget contribute to the medium you decide to use. LCD projection panels are fine for audiences of about 40 to 50. But 35mm slides are better for large auditorium-sized audiences. Overheads can look dim and dingy, and are often distorted when projected on a large screen. Electronic presentations are low resolution and appear faded compared to slides: They lack the sharp and crisp look of a slide. Video works well on a large screen; for speaker interaction it must be carefully planned for the purpose. Generally, these suggestions apply:

Use overheads:
- When you want audience interaction in a lighted room.
- For groups of no more than 35 to 40 people.
- When other equipment is not available.

Use 35mm slides:
- For any size audience, especially more than 50 people.
- For a non-interactive lecture presentation.
- For an interactive presentation; keep room semidarkened and use slide colors that project well with ambient light.

Use on-screen electronic presentations from a computer:
- For small audiences, depending on the projection unit size.
- For up to five people when using a laptop with a standard 14-inch or 17-inch monitor.
- For 25 to 50 people when using an LCD panel or projector.
- For up to 100 people when using a large-screen video projector and the room is not too large.
- For when you don't have time to produce slides or overheads.
- For when you want to interact with computer information using "whatever-ifs" or pre-programmed branching segments that can be accessed by buttons or keystrokes.
- For when you have pretested the system and are sure everything works as it should.

Use video:
- For a stand-alone presentation.
- For a planned speaker/video interactive presentation.

- With an appropriate audience for the monitor or projector size.
- With a large-screen video projector in a theater/auditorium-size group.

You'll also plan your presentation based on software capability. Presentation graphics programs such as Lotus Freelance®, Microsoft PowerPoint®, Aldus Persuasion®, Harvard Graphics®, and Gold Disk's Astound® have similar features with variations on the same theme. In one sense this has made it easier for speakers shopping for presentation software. The number of choices has grown, while the differences between those choices has shrunk, so that almost any program can be counted on to do a decent job. In another sense, the presenter's job has become harder. A few years ago, there were only a few choices; today there are more than two dozen presentation programs on the market.

Software doesn't produce content, you do. It supports the content visually; it helps drive your message home. Studies prove that people retain 70 percent of the information they both hear and see, compared to 20 percent of what they only hear, and 30 percent of what they only see.

Presentation packages are full-bodied products with numerous features. However, it is not necessary to use each color, type, font and feature in every visual. I've seen some visuals created for the first time on a computer where I was in sensory overload because so many colors and fonts were used. There are a few rules of design and layout that, when followed properly, can spare your audience from the most common design errors.

Show and tell
Each visual should address one of these questions: What is it? Where is it? How does it work? How much is there? All visuals, with the exception of text materials, should answer one of these questions. Otherwise, you probably don't need them.

Maintain legibility
Everything you show to an audience should be easily read from the worst seat in the room. Use type, lines, shapes and colors that work to clarify your message. There is never a good reason to confuse or frustrate your audience with small type or extraneous material. And just because you can get 66 lines of type on a piece of paper does not mean you should put it on your visual! The simpler, the better. If a few lines will effectively communicate your message, don't complicate your visuals.

Prioritize content
The form of each graphic should clarify the purpose for which it is used. The emphasis should be self-evident.

Provide an overview
The live presentation should communicate the "big picture." The handout materials should provide the "close-ups." The audience remembers concepts, trends and

impressions, not raw data or qualifying remarks.

Use illustrative information
Show pictures, diagrams and charts. Make your visuals memorable. It is the quality, not the quantity, of your visuals that counts.

Be consistent
Within any presentation, consistency will help clarify your use of the graphic language.

Know the limitations of your equipment
Design your materials to work within the limits of the proportion, size, color and resolution available on the output device. When multiple presentation media are to be used, design for the most restrictive medium or create multiple versions to satisfy the needs of each medium.

The 3M Meeting Management Institute released results of a study commissioned by the 3M Visual Systems Division and done at the University of Arizona. Previous 3M research, conducted by the University of Minnesota and the Wharton School of Business, University of Pennsylvania, laid the foundation for the latest study by identifying specific tools and techniques that improved audience perceptions of computer-gener-ated presentation graphics. The earlier research focused on black and white images vs. color, overhead trans-parencies vs. 35mm slides, and text vs. imagery. The earlier research concluded that presenters who use visuals in their presentations are perceived to be more professional, persuasive, and their meetings were of better quality – all good reasons to use visuals when you're presenting.

This study evaluated similar parameters, focusing on the impact of computer-based presentation systems. According to the new research, audiences respond best to a speaker who uses technology as a presentation aid. But response declines rapidly when the speaker takes a back seat to complex on-screen visuals that appear "canned" to the audience. The study recommends using computer-generated visuals to:

• Increase attention.
• Emphasize concepts on complex charts.
• Heighten the audience's perception of the presenter.

However, the study warns presenters to be cautious:

• Use animation with discretion to avoid sensory overload.
• Use transitions selectively to avoid overpowering the message.
• Use simple transitions to minimize audience distraction.
• Use transitions consistently to avoid confusion.

In a side study, researchers compared identical presentations given by two different speakers. The result: An average speaker using high-quality visuals can outperform a superior speaker using no visuals. While high-quality images can improve a presentation, however, they cannot compensate for an unprepared speaker with a poorly crafted message. In addition, simple color graphics, whether displayed on an overhead projector or 35mm slides or monitor, can be more effective than a "canned" multimedia presentation in which the presenter takes a back seat. Presenters cannot expect audience retention to improve automatically with graphics. Visuals are there to support you, the presenter, not replace you.

But, combine speaker charisma and podium presence with computer-generated visuals, and you'll have a powerhouse presentation that accomplishes your goals and gains high evaluations from everyone in attendance!

Sharon Adcock is principal of The Adcock Group, a consulting, speaking & training firm in Manhattan Beach, CA. She speaks frequently and has written numerous articles on visuals, technology, sales, marketing and presentations. She can be reached at (310) 545-9731 or Ski Adcock@aol.com

SUGGESTED READINGS

The following books and other learning tools were either used in preparation for *Speaking Is An Audience-Centered Sport*, or are simply good resources for speakers.

Tom Antion
WAKE 'EM UP! Business Presentations
Anchor Publishing

Peter Urs Bender
Secrets of Power Presentations
The Achievement Group

Dianna Booher
Executive's Portfolio of Model Speeches For All Occasions
Prentice Hall

Marjorie Brody, CSP & Shawn Kent
Power Presentations: How To Connect With Your Audience & Sell Your Ideas
John Wiley & Sons

Marjorie Brody, CSP
Speaking Your Way to the Top: Making Powerful Business Presentations
Allyn & Bacon

Marjorie Brody, CSP
"Present Like a Pro"
(videotape)

Marjorie Brody, CSP
"Present With Success"
(double audio cassette)

Marjorie Brody, CSP
"Power Presentations"
(computer software)

Tim Connor, CSP
Sales Mastery, Secrets of Six-Figure-Income Salespeople
Connor Resource Group

Jeff Scott Cook
The Elements of Speechwriting and Public Speaking
MacMillan

Joan Detz
How to Write and Give a Speech
St. Martin's Press

Eugene Ehrlich and Gene R. Hawes
Speak for Success
Bantam

Ron Hoff
I Can See You Naked
Andrews and McMeel

Karen Lawson, Ph.D., CSP
The Art of Influencing
Kendall Hunt

Thomas Leech
How to Prepare, Stage & Deliver Winning Presentations
AMACOM

Dona Z. Meilach
Looking Great on Video
Business One Irwin

Jim Meisenheimer
47 Ways To Sell Smarter
Helbern Publishing

Jim Meisenheimer
50 More Ways to Sell Smarter
Helbern Publishing

Laurie Schloff & Marcia Yudkin
Smart Speaking
Penguin Books

Sylvia Simmons
How To Be The Life of The Podium
AMACOM

Thomas K. Mira
The Princeton Review; Speak Smart; The Art of Public Speaking
Random House

Laurie E. Rozakis
The Complete Idiot's Guide to Speaking in Public With Confidence
Alpha Book

Christina Stuart
How to be an Effective Speaker
NTC Publishing Group

Philip R. Theibert
How to Give a Damn Good Speech
Career Press

Lilly Walters
Secrets of Successful Speakers
McGraw-Hill

Lilly Walters
What To Say When ... You're Dying on the Platform
McGraw-Hill

Dottie Walters & Lilly Walters
Speak and Grow Rich
Prentice Hall

Marion Witz
Stand Up and Talk to 1,000 People (and Enjoy it!)
McLeod Publishing

ABOUT BRODY COMMUNICATIONS LTD.

Brody Communications Ltd. trainers bring to your organization more than 40 years combined experience in oral communications training, speaking, coaching and writing. Marjorie Brody, CSP, and her associates have conducted successful seminars at major firms throughout the United States, Canada, Europe, Australia and the Middle East.

All Brody Communications Ltd. programs can be customized to meet specific corporate and participant needs.

Some of the programs that Brody Communications Ltd. offers include:

- Presentation Skills
  – Powerful Presentation Skills
  – Technical Presentation Skills
  – Sales Presentation Skills

- Executive Skills
  – Individual Coaching
  – Executive Speaking
  – Speech Writing
  – Video Assessment

- Management Development Skills
  – Conflict Management
  – Negotiation Skills
  – Networking Know-How
  – Team Building
  – Meetings That Work
  – Time/Stress Management

- Business Communication Skills
  - Business Etiquette Excellence
  - International Protocol & Presentation
  - Effective Business Writing
  - Interviewing Skills
  - The Art of Listening
  - Women in the Business World

- Training Techniques
  - Train-the-Trainer
  - Facilitator Training
  - Seminar Leadership
  - Group Dynamics

- Corporate Certification
  - Powerful Presentation Skills
  - Business Etiquette Excellence

- Keynote and Conference Speaking

All Brody Communications Ltd. associates are skilled speakers available for your keynotes, conferences, meetings and professional gatherings.

You can improve the communications skills of your corporate personnel. To schedule seminars at your firm or for more information on our offerings, call 215-886-1688.

ABOUT MARJORIE BRODY, CSP
SPEAKER/AUTHOR/EXECUTIVE COACH

As the founder and president of Brody Communications Ltd., Marjorie Brody wears four hats: company president, professional speaker, trainer/executive coach, and published author.

In her role as president, Marjorie has taken her vision of how presentation and business communication skills could best be taught, and developed customized programs for a range of corporations and individuals.

As an internationally recognized speaker, Marjorie proudly wears the designation of CSP, Certified Speaking Professional, one of only a handful of speakers so designated by the National Speakers Association. Marjorie travels extensively as a trainer/executive coach, sharing her knowledge with people in the United States and abroad conducting seminars/workshops on presentation skills, business etiquette, personal marketing, and networking. Through repeat business and referrals, she has built up an impressive client roster of *Fortune* 100 and 500 companies.

A well-published writer and author, Marjorie Brody co-authored or authored the books *21 Ways to Springboard Your Speaking, Training & Consulting Career* (Career Skills Press), *Power Presentations* (Wiley & Sons), *Complete Business Etiquette Handbook* (Prentice Hall), *Business Etiquette* (McGraw-Hill), *Climbing The Corporate Ladder* (SkillPath), and *Minding Your Business Manners* (SkillPath). Her newest book is *Speaking Your Way to the Top: Making*

Powerful Business Presentations (Allyn & Bacon).

Marjorie has three double-cassette audio programs: "Present With Success," "Up Your E.Q. (Etiquette Quotient)," and "21 Ways To Springboard Your Speaking, Training & Consulting Career," and a four-cassette series, "Finishing First: The Promotable Person's Guide to Success in a Competitive World." Marjorie also has a video, "Present Like a Pro," and computer software called "Power Presentations." Marjorie is profiled on several speaking- and training-related sites on the Internet's World Wide Web, and has a home page for Brody Communications Ltd.: http://www.brodycomm.com .

Member: National Speakers Association, Liberty Bell Speakers Association (President 1997/98), American Society for Training & Development, Master Speakers International

Interesting Facts: Best-selling author; subject of numerous TV, radio and print interviews; Liberty Bell Speakers Association Chapter Member of the Year (1997); Professor Emeritus, Bucks County Community College; Affiliate Member, International Association for Continuing Education and Training; International Who's Who of Professionals; 2,000 Notable American Women

Presentations: Market Your Magic, Seeds For Success, Professional Etiquette, Present Like a Pro

BRODY COMMUNICATIONS LTD. LEARNING TOOLS

Books

1) Marjorie Brody, CSP & Shawn Kent
Power Presentations: How To Connect With Your Audience & Sell Your Ideas
$19.95, John Wiley & Sons

2) Marjorie Brody, CSP
Speaking Your Way to the Top: Making Powerful Business Presentations
$15, Allyn & Bacon

3) Marjorie Brody, CSP
21 Ways to Springboard Your Speaking, Training & Consulting Career
$14.95, Career Skills Press

4) Marjorie Brody, CSP & Barbara Pachter
Complete Business Etiquette Handbook
$29.95, Prentice Hall

5) Marjorie Brody, CSP & Barbara Pachter
Business Etiquette
$10, McGraw-Hill Publishing

6) Marjorie Brody, CSP & Barbara Pachter
Minding Your Business Manners
$10.95, SkillPath

7) Marjorie Brody, CSP & Barbara Pachter
Climbing The Corporate Ladder
$15.95, SkillPath

Audio Cassettes

8) Marjorie Brody, CSP & Barbara Pachter
"Finishing First: The Promotable Person's Guide To Success in a Competitive World"
(four audio cassettes, $39.95, SkillPath)

9) Marjorie Brody, CSP
"Present With Success"
(double audio cassette, $18.95)

10) *"21 Ways To Springboard Your Speaking, Training & Consulting Career"*
(double audio cassette, $18.95)

11) Marjorie Brody, CSP & Barbara Pachter
"Up Your E.Q." (Etiquette Quotient)
(double audio cassette, $18.95)

Video $39.95

12) Marjorie Brody, CSP
"Present Like a Pro"

Software $24.95

13) Marjorie Brody, CSP
"Power Presentations"
(PC only)

Special Reports $4.50 each

14) *"Effective Business Writing"*
15) *"Effective Sales Presentations"*
16) *"Making & Using Visual Aids"*
17) *"Market Your MAGIC"*
18) *"Networking: The Word May Be Overused,
     But The Skills Are Essential"*
19) *"Putting Together Your Business Wardrobe"*
20) *"Strategies for Effective Meetings"*
21) *"25 Ways to Navigate the Business Meal"*

Order Form

Mail: Brody Communications Ltd.
P.O. Box 8868
Elkins Park, PA 19027
FAX: 215-886-1699

Please rush me:

Item#	Unit Price	Quantity	Total

Subtotal:

Tax: (PA residents add 6%, Phila. 7%)

Shipping & Handling: ($4.25 1st item, $1 each additional item; $1 special report, $.50 each additional)

Total:

Name:_____Company:_____
Address: _____
City/State/Zip:_____
Phone: _____FAX:_____

Check or Money order (payable to Brody Communications Ltd.)
Credit Card: Visa   Master Card   (circle one)
Account Number:_____
Exp. Date:_____
Signature:_____